Animals
in the
Classroom
Selection, Care, and Observations

David C. Kramer
St. Cloud State University

▲▼ Addison-Wesley Publishing Company

Menlo Park, California • Reading, Massachusetts • New York
Don Mills, Ontario • Wokingham, England • Amsterdam • Bonn
Sydney • Singapore • Tokyo • Madrid • San Juan

Acknowledgments

This book is published by the Addison-Wesley Innovative Division.

Design: Leigh McLellen
Cover Design: Daniel Frazier
Illustrations: Marlene Howerton
Photographs: 13 Stephen Frisch*; 33 Jeff Korte/Learning Resources Services, St. Cloud State University; 40 Hans Reinhard/Bruce Coleman Inc.; 41 Runk-Schoenberger/Grant Heilman Photography; 48 Dan Marek/Learning Resources Services, St. Cloud State University; 53 Runk-Schoenberger/Grant Heilman Photography; 58 Grant Heilman/ Grant Heilman Photography; 59 Grant Heilman/Grant Heilman Photography; 63 John Markham/Bruce Coleman Inc.; 64 USDA; 68 USDA; 73 Mike Mazzaschi/Stock, Boston; 75 Oxford Scientific Films/Animals, Animals; 79 Terry Ashley/Tom Stack & Associates; 84 Runk-Schoenberger/Grant Heilman Photography; 90 D. J. Lyons/Bruce Coleman Inc.; 97 Mark Tuschman*; 101 Mark Tuschman*; 106 John Coulter/Learning Resources Services, St. Cloud State University; 110 Runk-Schoenberger/Grant Heilman Photography; 118 Barry L. Runk/Grant Heilman Photography; 122 John Coulter/Learning Resource Services, St. Cloud State University; 126 Runk-Schoenberger/Grant Heilman Photography; 131 David C. Kramer; 135 G. E. Hyde/Bruce Coleman Inc.; 142 Jen & Des Bartlett/Bruce Coleman; 144 John Coulter/Learning Resources Services, St. Cloud State University; 149 New York Zoological Society; 153 John Coulter/Learning Resources Services, St. Cloud State University; 157 Runk-Schoenberger/Grant Heilman Photography; 163 David C. Kramer; 168 Leonard Lee Rue III/Bruce Coleman Inc.; 171 Dan Marek & Jeff Korte/Learning Resources Services, St. Cloud State University; 176 Runk-Schoenberger/Grant Heilman Photography; 181 Wayland Lee*/Addison-Wesley Publishing Company; 187 Dan Marek & Jeff Korte/Learning Resources Services, St. Cloud State University; 193 Dan Marek & Jeff Korte/Learning Resources Services, St. Cloud State University; 199 Dan Marek & Jeff Korte/Learning Resources Services, St. Cloud State University; 205 Hans Reinhard/Bruce Coleman Inc.; 211 Grant Heilman/Grant Heilman Photography; 216 Jane Burton/Bruce Coleman Inc.

All other photographs taken expressly for the publisher by Elliott Smith.

*Photographs taken expressly for the publisher.

ISBN 0–201–20679–X

5 6 7 8 9 10 - ML - 95 94 93

Preface

I cannot remember a time when I was not interested in animals. As a child, this interest was characterized by numerous jars of captive insects and spiders that found their way into our home. Later, frogs, toads, salamanders, snakes, and turtles were added to the menagerie. At one time or another, I have kept pigeons, quails, and pheasants, as well as a variety of domestic animals, such as chickens, lambs, and pigs.

Although I was not especially academically oriented at the time, keeping these animals successfully demanded that I develop knowledge of their habits, thereby encouraging study that might not otherwise have occurred. Keeping the animals in captivity also provided an opportunity to observe them closely and to learn to care about them and their well-being. This early interest persisted and resulted in a career that has been both enjoyable and satisfying. As a teacher, I am able to share my interests with others. As a teacher of prospective teachers, I encourage my students to capitalize on the natural curiosity of children and to stimulate their interest by keeping animals in the classroom. In doing so, some of the children may develop, as I did, a long-term interest in animals, and perhaps all will learn to appreciate the place of animals in the world.

Animals in the Classroom has three goals. The first is to encourage teachers to stimulate student curiosity and interest in learning about animals by keeping live animals in their classrooms. The second goal is to assist teachers in selecting appropriate classroom animals and caring for them in a humane way. The third goal is to provide sufficient information to allow teachers to answer students' questions confidently and to provide meaningful learning experiences with a variety of classroom animals.

Although many animals can be kept in the classroom, this book discusses twenty-eight that represent various levels of the animal kingdom. I have personally kept all of these animals under the classroom conditions described in the book. About half of the information in the book describes where and how each animal lives in nature. The remaining information describes the animals' care and maintenance in the classroom and includes suggestions for student observations and activities. All of these animals can be kept in more sophisticated ways, but the techniques recommended are simple methods that work and that ensure humane treatment of the animals.

I am especially appreciative to those who made it possible for me to pursue and complete this project: my mother, who tolerated more jars and cages in and around the house than she probably should have; Dr. James C. List, who encouraged me more than he knows; Dr. John

Coulter, who taught me about teaching; Phil Tennison, who gave me continual encouragement and understanding; and my wife, Joan, who continues to tolerate the jars and cages, as well as me and my perpetual piles of books and papers, in the kitchen. I also wish to express my appreciation for the photographic assistance of John Coulter, Jeff Korte, Dan Marek, and Mike Nelson. Finally, it should be noted that some of the material in this book was previously published in *Science and Children,* a publication of the National Science Teachers Association. I sincerely appreciate NSTA's support.

About the Author

David C. Kramer is Professor of Biology and Science Education at St. Cloud State University (Minnesota) and a former junior high school science teacher. Dr. Kramer also conducts frequent workshops and courses for inservice teachers in nature study, environmental education, science education, and the care of animals in the classroom. He has written numerous articles on science education and has been a regular contributor to the popular animal care and maintenance column "The Classroom Animal" in *Science and Children,* a publication of the National Science Teachers Association.

Contents

Part 1 Keeping Animals in the Classroom

Animal study is a worthwhile enterprise for children. In the past, primitive human societies relied on animals for food, clothing, and shelter. At that time, human survival depended on a knowledge of animals and their ways. Later, more organized agrarian societies relied less on animals for day-to-day existence but still depended on them for food, transportation, and income. Although animals are still a source of food and other products, our survival no longer depends on each individual's having knowledge of them. However, because animals are a part of our cultural heritage and continue to be an important part of our lives, it is appropriate that children have the opportunity to experience, know, and appreciate them.

Animals can be studied in a variety of ways, but keeping them in the classroom and studying them at close range is one of the more stimulating approaches. If, according to the ancient Chinese proverb, "a picture is worth a thousand words," then the opportunity to see a live animal, care for it, and perhaps hold it, must be worth a thousand more. Seeing an animal move, eat, or care for its young would certainly increase a child's knowledge and experience far beyond that afforded by words, a picture, or a film. As for appreciation, elusive as it is, one might rightly assume that it would also increase as knowledge and experience increase.

Almost any animal kept in the classroom—whether it's a toad, a spider, or a gerbil—will provide interesting and stimulating learning experiences for students. Children are fascinated by animals and can, through their own observations, discover many things about a classroom animal, such as its size, shape, color and markings, number of legs, number of body parts, eating habits, and behavior. When a teacher brings an animal into the class-

room, students will ask numerous questions: Where does it live in nature? What does it eat and how much? How big will it get? Does it bite? What kind of cage does it need? How can we make it comfortable? Who will care for it? These and other questions can provide the basis for classroom discussions, individual student projects, or projects for the entire class, particularly if a number of animals are involved.

Keeping animals in the classroom is more than just an interesting way to learn about individual animals; it is also educationally sound. It is consistent with the goals of most elementary or middle school science programs and with what is known about how children learn. If properly approached, it can play an important role in helping children to learn and understand ecological concepts, develop a sense of responsibility, and develop positive attitudes toward living things.

<table>
| Chapter | **1** | *Planning a Live-Animal Project* |
</table>

Chapter 1   *Planning a Live-Animal Project*

While many types of animals can be kept successfully in the classroom and provide valuable educational experiences for students, several factors should be considered before acquiring any animal and embarking on such a venture. As with all worthwhile educational endeavors, planning is essential. A well-planned live-animal project is more likely to provide meaningful learning experiences for students, as well as be more satisfying for the teacher. It is also essential for the welfare of the animal involved.

In planning to keep live animals in the classroom, teachers should consider the following:

• the educational goals of the project
• the responsibilities involved
• selecting and obtaining appropriate animals
• the legal considerations
• student health and safety
• animal health and environment
• what to do with the animals when the project is over

These considerations are interrelated; each affects or is affected by the others. Each consideration, as well as related issues, is discussed separately in the following pages.

Educational Goals

One of the first steps in planning to keep a classroom animal is to establish the goals of the project. There are many valid reasons for keeping animals in the classroom, but the primary one should be to provide meaningful educational experiences for students. A live-animal project might be undertaken in order to stimulate interest, illustrate certain biological or ecological principles, develop or improve observational skills, foster a sense of empathy, promote positive attitudes, or any number of other reasons. Whatever the goals, they should be determined at the outset and kept clearly in mind, governing other aspects of the project, such as selecting appropriate animals and evaluating student learning.

Responsibilities

The responsibilities involved in keeping an animal in the classroom are extensive and varied, but the most important responsibility is the proper care of the animal. A captive animal is totally dependent on its keeper, who assumes the responsibility for providing food and shelter and for ensuring that the animal is healthy, comfortable, and able to practice its natural behavior. The keeper must also consistently demonstrate to students a caring, sensitive attitude toward the animal. And, of course, the responsibility for providing a safe learning environment and meaningful learning experiences for students is as applicable when dealing with animals as it is with any other educational endeavor.

Selecting and Obtaining Animals

Selecting Animals   One of the most important decisions in planning a classroom animal project is selecting an appropriate species. Obviously, the educational goals of the project should provide guidelines for this determination. However, not all animals that might meet these criteria are appropriate for all educational settings, and some animals are not suitable to keep in the classroom at all. In selecting an animal for the classroom, the teacher should consider the health and safety of the students; any legal limitations;

the health of the animal; the food, water, housing, and space requirements of the animal; and the day-to-day care required to maintain the animal in an appropriate way. Each of these factors is important and is discussed further, but the teacher should also consider the following generalizations about animals in the classroom:

1. Smaller animals are generally better than larger ones.
2. Local animals are generally better than exotic ones.
3. Wild mammals should not be kept in the classroom.
4. Venomous animals should not be kept in the classroom.
5. Sick or injured animals should not be kept in the classroom.
6. No animal should be kept in the classroom unless:
    • it is hardy and can thrive in captivity
    • its natural habitat can be duplicated there
    • its normal behavior can be expressed in the enclosure
    • it can adjust to the normal classroom environment
    • it can be properly cared for over weekends

Obtaining Animals   Classroom animals can sometimes be collected locally from their natural habitats or purchased from a pet store or a biological supply company. (See Resources, page 226.) Pet owners are also sometimes willing, even anxious, to donate unwanted animals, especially ones from large or unexpected litters. However, indiscriminate collecting of animals should be discouraged, and students should be instructed *not* to pick up any animal and bring it into the classroom. If local animals are collected, the collection should be done sparingly and selectively—only the desired species—and the animals should be captured and transported in a way that will not harm them. Pets offered to the school should be accepted only if their presence in the classroom is consistent with the educational objectives of the program and if they meet the other acceptable criteria. Regardless of how an animal is obtained, it is important to identify it accurately, as this will determine the animal's suitability for the classroom and how it should be cared for.

Legal Considerations

Some native animals—especially fur-bearing animals, most birds, and threatened or endangered species—are protected by federal or state regulations and cannot be collected or maintained without a permit. Federal regulations also prohibit importation of some animals, and some states prohibit importing or keeping certain animals that might become established or cause ecological damage if they escaped or were released. Your state wildlife agency will be familiar with these regulations and can provide information on animals having protected status in your district. (See page 227 for the agency's address.) In addition, some school districts have rules or recommendations concerning classroom animals. In this case, the principal or science coordinator will be familiar with any such regulations. Obviously, illegal or banned animals should not be brought into the classroom.

Student Health and Safety

Student health and safety is always an important consideration when selecting and keeping classroom animals. Some animals bite, sting, or carry diseases that can be transmitted to humans. While this fact should not preclude keeping animals, it does mean that teachers should take appropriate and sensible precautions. Potentially dangerous animals, such as venomous reptiles and insects or wild mammals, should never be brought into the classroom. Even nonvenomous animals can sometimes bite or scratch, and teachers should be aware of this when planning to keep a classroom animal.

Insect bites and stings, although usually not harmful, can be painful. Some spiders especially can cause painful, slow-healing wounds. In addition, some children are hypersensitive, particularly to stings, and should not be exposed to them. However, insect bites and stings and spider bites can usually be prevented through proper handling.

Occasionally, a student might have an allergic reaction to a certain kind of animal or to dust from the cage. If so, the animal should not be kept in the classroom.

Certain diseases can be transmitted from animals to humans, either directly (through bites or handling) or indirectly (from airborne organisms). This problem is primarily associated with turtles, certain birds, and some mammals taken from the wild. The risk of disease can be reduced by keeping only healthy animals and by attending to their hygiene. And students should always wash their hands before and after feeding the animals, handling them, or cleaning their cages. Because of the possibility of disease, any animal bite should receive prompt medical attention, and the animal should be retained for testing.

Animal Health and Environment

Animal Health   Only healthy animals should be selected for the classroom, but even an animal that appears to be healthy can become ill; and teachers should constantly be alert to this possibility. Diagnosing animal disease is beyond the expertise of most classroom teachers, but certain general symptoms—such as a change in behavior, lethargy, loss of appetite or weight, or respiratory problems—are easily noticed and can indicate health-related problems. If any animal becomes ill or shows signs of disease, it should not be kept in the classroom. A sick animal should be isolated from other animals and kept in a quiet place where it can be cared for until an appropriate course of action can be determined. The animal may recover on its own with normal care or a veterinarian may need to be consulted. In some cases, euthanasia (painless killing) may be necessary. Although the thought of euthanasia is unpleasant, especially to anyone who cares about animals, it is sometimes the best course of action. A veterinarian or the local humane organization should be consulted if the need arises.

Food and Feeding   A good diet, consisting of proper food in adequate amounts, is essential to the health of any animal. It is therefore best to offer a captive animal its natural food, insofar as this is possible. Food can be collected from the animal's natural environment or purchased from a pet store or bait shop. However, natural foods that are abundant during one season might not be available at another time, and this should be considered in determining whether a certain animal can be kept and for how long.

Some natural foods—such as earthworms, crickets, mealworms, fruit flies, and daphnia—can be raised in the classroom. The chart below shows some classroom animals that will eat these natural foods.

Animals That Will Eat:

Earthworms

Toads
Salamanders
Leopard Frogs
Box Turtles
Painted Turtles
Garter Snakes

Crickets

Toads
Tree Frogs
Leopard Frogs
Salamanders
Anoles
Box Turtles

Mealworms

Toads
Tree Frogs
Leopard Frogs
Salamanders
Anoles
Box Turtles
Painted Turtles

Fruit Flies

Praying Mantises
Anoles
Web-Spinning Spiders

Daphnia

Tiger Salamander Larvae
Guppies

Substitute foods are satisfactory if the animal will accept them and if they meet its nutritional requirements. But, in general, part of the decision to keep any animal is determining whether an appropriate food supply will be available on a continuing basis.

Many animals vary their food intake at different times of the year, and some might refuse to eat for relatively long periods. Some books recommend techniques for force-feeding animals, but this should be completely avoided. Unless the animal appears ill, it is best to offer the proper food and let the animal decide whether it needs to eat or not.

Water   All living things need water. Although some animals obtain what they need indirectly through their food or environment and rarely or never drink, it is essential to provide all captive animals with a source of water. For those animals that will use them, inverted water bottles are best as they are not likely to spill and are easy to refill and clean. Some animals will lick water droplets from a sprinkled plant, while others will take water from a soaked sponge. Others prefer an open container in which they can drink and soak. The method of supplying water will depend on the kind of animal being kept, which is another important reason for knowing its habits.

Housing   The kind of enclosure required will vary considerably, depending on the type of animal and its environmental needs. A multipurpose cage or a screen-covered aquarium will meet the needs of many animals. Even wide-mouthed jars are useful for small specimens, such as spiders and insects. However, there are several factors to consider in selecting a cage for each type of animal. Foremost are the needs and comfort of the animal. The cage chosen should be large enough to provide adequate exercise space, have good ventilation, and, for most specimens, have a hiding place. It should have an adequate food and water delivery system and an adequate opening to allow for maintenance (including cleaning). The cage should also be secure to prevent escapes. Finally, since the primary purpose for keeping a classroom animal is to allow students to observe it, the cage, if not transparent, should have a window or viewing panel. (Chapter 2 discusses cages, equipment, and environments in greater detail.)

Cleanliness   Good hygiene is important for two reasons. First, other than a proper diet, nothing is more important to an animal's health, comfort, and well-being than a clean environment. Second, probably few things reflect an attitude toward an animal, either positive or negative, more than the quality of the care it is given. It is therefore imperative that the animal be kept in a clean, pleasant environment—both for the welfare of the animal and for the important lesson that is demonstrated to students.

Day-to-day Care   A certain amount of time and attention is required to keep any animal in the classroom, and some animals require considerably more effort than others. Teachers should find out, then, what kind of care is required and avoid those animals that require more special attention and facilities than are feasible. Students can be given some responsibility for an animal's care, if they are properly supervised. This will not only free the teacher of the task but will also enrich the students' experience.

Caring for animals on weekends and vacations poses special problems, and this should be considered in the selection process. Animals that can be left unattended with a supply of food and water are easier to deal with than those that require daily attention. However, some teachers have found that sending animals home with students for weekend or vacation visits can resolve the problem. This, of course, should be done only with parental approval.

Be Prepared   A teacher never knows when an animal might arrive in the classroom. A specimen might be picked up on the playground during recess, brought from home in a pocket or a jar, or dropped off at school by a well-meaning person, especially when students or community members know of a teacher's interest in animals. These unexpected deliveries should be discouraged to prevent indiscriminate collecting and to promote responsible thinking about animal welfare. However, if animals do arrive unexpectedly, they must be dealt with immediately. Sometimes, depending on the type of animal, they can simply be released outdoors. Other times, they will need to be housed temporarily until they can be dealt with in a more permanent way. Keep a multipurpose cage and a screen-covered jar or two for these unexpected guests.

When the Project Is Over

When the animals are no longer wanted or needed in the classroom, they must still be dealt with in a responsible way. Animals that have been collected locally can be released back into their natural habitats, provided that the weather has not changed significantly. However, animals that are not native to a given area or animals that have been purchased (even if they are thought to be native to the area) should *not* be released. Non-native animals released into the local area may suffer and die if the environment is inappropriate. If they survive and become established, they can create serious ecological and environmental damage. Sometimes an animal can be given to someone who will be responsible for its care, perhaps another teacher who can also use it for educational purposes. Many times, students will want to take a classroom animal home as a personal pet; but, of course, this should only be permitted with parental approval and if it is certain that both the child and the parent are knowledgeable about the animal's needs. A pet store might also accept (and will sometimes purchase) a healthy animal for resale. The store might also be interested in insects, such as crickets or mealworms, that can be used as food for other animals.

Other Considerations

Although children are generally fascinated by animals, they do not all share the same enthusiasm for being in close contact with them. Teachers should be especially sensitive to these feelings. Negative feelings are usually mild and quickly forgotten if the animals are carefully introduced to students. Occasionally, however, a student might have strong negative feelings about certain animals, and this should be respected. These feelings are real and will not be overcome by ridicule or embarrassment or by forcing a student to touch an animal.

Many children will want to hold an animal, and the experience can be a positive one for the students. However, being picked up and held is not natural for an animal, and being passed around a class of thirty students could be a frightening experience for a small animal. Furthermore, animals and children are easily excited and can surprise each other with a quick movement; the result can be a frightened animal loose in the classroom. To make handling a more positive experience for both students and the animal, the animal should be picked up properly and held securely. Handling periods should be limited to only a few minutes at a time.

Whatever the reasons for keeping animals in the classroom, it is in the best interest of the animals not to keep them there longer than necessary to achieve the educational goals of the project. Native animals should be kept for only one or two weeks. Many animals that are normally kept in confinement, such as gerbils, hamsters, and guinea pigs, can be kept in the classroom for longer periods of time. It is also best if the animals are released or removed from the classroom before students lose interest in them and care becomes a burden.

Chapter 2 Cages, Equipment, and Environments

Each kind of animal has its own unique combination of environmental requirements that include habitat, food, water, and climate. An animal's comfort in captivity, and perhaps its survival, depends to a great extent on the degree to which these needs are provided for or simulated. In this regard, a cage is more than simply a structure for confining an animal. It is an environmental chamber—a means of providing for an animal's needs through the use of cage equipment such as food and water containers, an activity wheel, a nest box, and substrate materials. Adequate space, light intensity, temperature, and humidity are also important considerations, and these can be provided or controlled by the selection and use of a proper cage and other supplementary equipment.

Several kinds of cages, equipment, and environmental factors will be referred to repeatedly in later chapters as individual animals are discussed. For expediency, they are described here for general information and subsequent reference.

Cages

The cage is the most important piece of equipment for keeping a classroom animal. From the keeper's perspective, the enclosure should have easy access for providing food and water and for general care and cleaning. Since the animal project is intended to be a learning experience, the cage should also provide good visibility for the observer. From the animal's perspective, the cage should provide for all of its basic needs and be as comfortable as possible. Several kinds of specialty or multipurpose cages can be purchased, and others can be constructed, but no single kind of cage meets the needs of all animals. It is also not always possible to meet all of an animal's needs as well as the desires of the keeper, so some compromise might be necessary. If so, the compromise should be in favor of the well-being of the animal.

A standard aquarium is probably one of the most versatile cages because it can be used to simulate a wide variety of environments. Its use as an aquatic environment is obvious, but, fitted with an appropriate cover, it can also be used to simulate several different terrestrial environments or an aquarium-terrarium combination. Equipped in yet other ways, it can be a useful cage for a variety of small animals. Aquariums are available in a range of sizes and can usually be purchased at local pet shops.

Aquarium

While normally thought of as an environment for fish, an aquarium is simply a cage that simulates a pond or a lake. As such, it can also be used to house a variety of other aquatic organisms, including certain turtles, amphibians, insects, snails, and crayfish. In its simplest form, an aquarium need only be filled with water, an inch or two (2.5–5 cm) of sand or gravel, and a few aquatic plants to meet the needs of some aquatic animals (including some fish). This basic environment can be modified to accommodate the needs of a variety of other aquatic organisms through the use of lights, a filter, and

Figure 2-1 Aquarium

a heater. The need for these items will depend on the type of animal being kept and will be discussed under "equipment" in this chapter. (Chapter 6 discusses in detail aquariums and the aquatic environment and describes three levels of aquariums for fish. See pages 101–105.)

Planted Terrarium

A planted terrarium is an ideal way to house a variety of small animals, such as tree frogs and lizards, because it is possible to almost exactly duplicate their natural environments. This has a great deal of aesthetic appeal for the observer and provides an opportunity to observe the animal in its natural environment. It also provides a comfortable home for the captive. Some moist soil, a piece of a log or stump, a rock, a branching twig, and a handful of leaves can be arranged, along with suitable plants, to simulate a forest floor environment. Watering the plants appropriately will keep the soil

Figure 2-2 Planted terrarium

moist and help maintain the humidity. A glass cover will reduce evaporation and maintain an even higher humidity level. Different plants, a gravel substrate, and a screen cover will create a desert environment. Of course, the environment, including the type of plants used, should be consistent with the kind of animal being kept.

While useful for some animals, a planted terrarium is not without certain problems if used for others. Some animals, especially larger snakes and turtles, will crawl over or climb the plants and crush them. Some animals will even eat the plants. Burrowing animals, such as toads, salamanders, and some turtles, will be out of view much of the time and will possibly uproot the plants. A planted terrarium is also difficult to clean, especially if the animal is a messy eater or produces large amounts of wastes.

Modified Terrarium

The modified terrarium is very similar to the planted terrarium except that the plants are kept in pots. With this arrangement, the plants can easily be removed and replaced if needed, and they will not be uprooted by any burrowing activity. Also, less substrate material is needed since the plants are not rooted in it; as a result, burrowing animals will be more visible. Of course, an appropriate cover (glass or screen) will be needed to confine certain animals and to help maintain the proper environment.

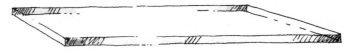

Figure 2-3   Modified terrarium

Sterile Terrarium

The sterile terrarium, so named because it does not contain any living things other than the captive, is used primarily for housing snakes. It has less aesthetic appeal and does not simulate a specific environment, but it solves some of the problems of other terrariums. The substrate can be several thicknesses of paper towel, which can easily be removed and replaced to clean the cage. A long forked stick wedged between one corner and the opposite sides of the cage or a large rock will provide a place for climbing, basking, or rubbing. A screen cover is best for this type of cage.

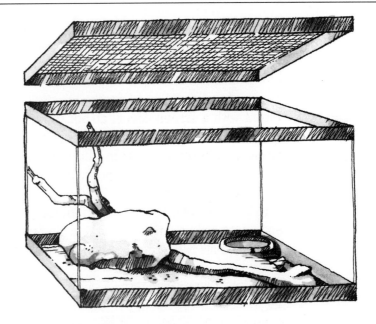

Figure 2-4   Sterile terrarium

Combination Aquarium-Terrarium

The combination aquarium-terrarium provides both a terrestrial and an aquatic environment, allowing the animal to move freely from one to the other. It is ideal for semiaquatic animals, such as frogs, toads, and salamanders. To simulate this environment, many sourcebooks recommend placing soil or gravel in one end of an aquarium and water in the other. However, this arrangement has several drawbacks. The soil becomes waterlogged and muddy, and most plants do not do well in it. The soil is often carried into the water, and it is not possible to change the water without disturbing the entire arrangement. A much more practical and satisfactory method is to use a wide, shallow water bowl (such as a flower pot holder) or a pan for the pond. It can be partially recessed in the soil to provide easy access for the animal. And, of course, the bowl can be easily removed for

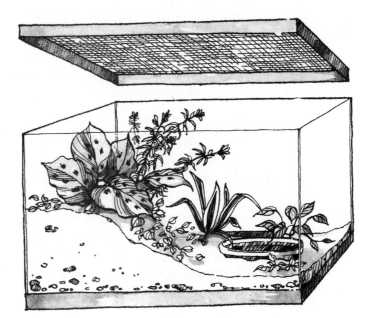

Figure 2-5   Combination aquarium-terrarium

cleaning. Either a glass or a screen cover should be used on the aquarium-terrarium, depending on the kind of animal being kept and the type of environment desired.

Small Animal Cage

Fitted with a screen cover, an aquarium is a satisfactory cage for a wide variety of small- to medium-sized animals, such as mice, gerbils, hamsters, snakes, and even insects. In fact, many aquariums are sold with a screen cover expressly for this purpose. If a cover is not available, one can easily be made by attaching a piece of ¼-inch or ½-inch hardware cloth or screen wire to a wooden frame (1″ x 2″ lumber is about right) that is just large enough to slide over the aquarium. So fitted, an aquarium can be used for those animals requiring a cage with a solid bottom.

Figure 2-6   Small animal cage

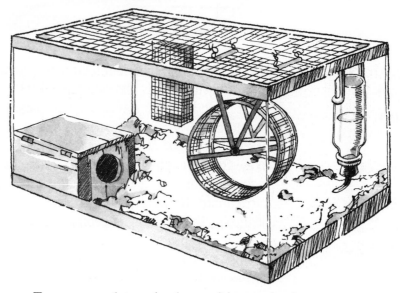

To accommodate animals requiring a wire-bottom cage, another piece of ½-inch hardware cloth can be attached to a wooden frame (also made of 1″ x 2″ lumber) that will fit snugly into the aquarium. Droppings that fall through the wire screen can be caught on layers of newspaper, which can be easily changed, or a shallow plastic tray can be placed below the wire bottom to catch the wastes.

Multipurpose Cages

The multipurpose cages illustrated in Figures 2-7, 2-8, and 2-9 can easily be constructed in a home or school workshop. These cages can be made in a variety of sizes and modified as needed to suit a specific animal. The cage illustrated in Figure 2-7 is an especially practical and versatile style for small mammals and birds. It is made of plywood and has a ½-inch hardware cloth bottom to allow wastes to fall through. It has a pull-out tray for easy cleaning and a large door for access. It can also be modified in several ways. For example, the top can be hinged for access rather than having a front door; a glass, plastic, or wire panel can replace one side for greater visibility; a

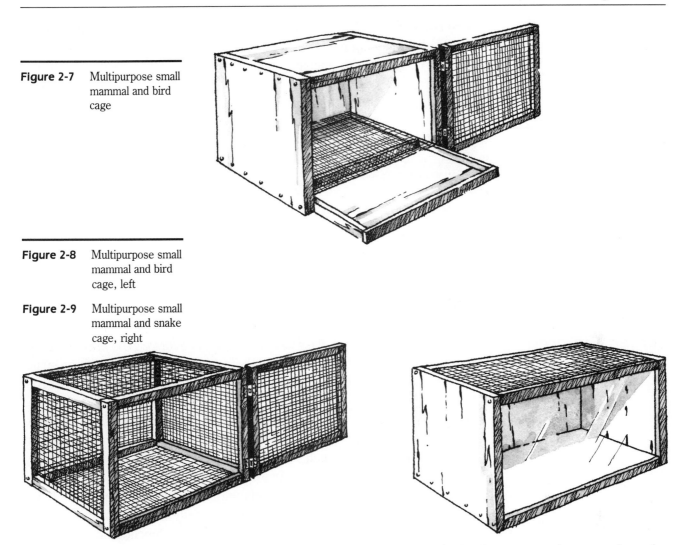

Figure 2-7   Multipurpose small mammal and bird cage

Figure 2-8   Multipurpose small mammal and bird cage, left

Figure 2-9   Multipurpose small mammal and snake cage, right

piece of galvanized metal (available in hardware stores) or wood can be placed over the screen bottom to accommodate animals requiring a solid bottom; or legs can be attached so that the cage can stand on the floor. The wire-covered wood frame cage shown in Figure 2-8 is useful for birds such as doves and for some small mammals. The cage shown in Figure 2-9 is basically a wooden box with a glass front and can be fitted with a solid or screen top. It is especially useful for snakes but will also accommodate some small mammals, such as mice, gerbils, or hamsters.

CAUTION: Care should be taken to ensure that homemade cages are free from potentially harmful substances, such as wood preservatives, paints, and adhesives, and that there are no sharp edges or protruding nails that might cause injury to an animal.

Commercial Rodent Cage

Commercial rodent cages are designed for smaller mammals, such as mice, rats, gerbils, and hamsters. These plastic cages are durable, provide good visibility, and are available in a variety of sizes. A primary advantage of this kind of cage is the ease with which the animals in it can be maintained. The wire cover holds a water bottle and a supply of food, both of which can be provided without opening the cage. Cleaning the cage involves simply lifting the lid, removing the animals, and pouring out and replacing the litter. These cages are available through biological supply companies (see Resources, page 226) but are rather expensive.

Figure 2-10   Commercial rodent cage

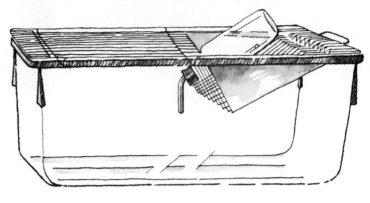

Screen-Covered Jar

One-quart or one-gallon glass jars with screen covers can be used either as temporary quarters for holding or viewing smaller animals, such as snails and mealworms, or as permanent housing for insects and other invertebrates. Canning jars with ring lids are especially useful for this purpose. The metal insert in the lid can be replaced with screen wire or a hole-punched plastic disk (cut from a margarine tub cover or a coffee can lid and punched with a paper punch). Jars can be as versatile as aquariums if they are set up to simulate various environments.

CAUTION: Do not use metal lids with nail-punched holes. Nail holes punched in metal jar lids are sharp and potentially dangerous. Punched inward, they can cause serious injury to an animal. Punched outward, they can cut fingers.

Figure 2-11   Screen-covered jar

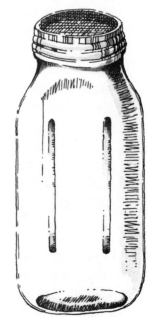

Equipment and Environments

A cage provides the beginning of an appropriate environment for an animal. The animal's remaining environmental needs can be provided for or controlled with a variety of other equipment and materials, which are often essential to an animal's well-being. The specific needs of animals vary, but the means of providing for them are normally relatively simple. The items described here are available in pet stores and from most biological supply companies or can be easily constructed.

Providing Food

Whenever possible, food should be provided in such a way that it will not be spilled in the cage or fouled by animal wastes and cage litter. The types of feeding equipment shown in Figures 2-12, 2-13, 2-14, and 2-15 will help avoid these problems. To prevent spills, food and water bowls should be made of heavy material or be designed to minimize tipping (see Figure 2-12). Dog and cat food dishes are useful for many animals. Alternatively, the food container can be attached to the side of the cage. A gravity-flow food hopper (Figure 2-13) is useful for some animals that eat grain or pellets. It holds a large food supply but makes only a small amount available at a given time. Another approach that works nicely for mice and rats is to let them gnaw at food suspended in a wire basket (see Figure 2-14). A chick feeder (Figure 2-15) meets the needs of most bird species.

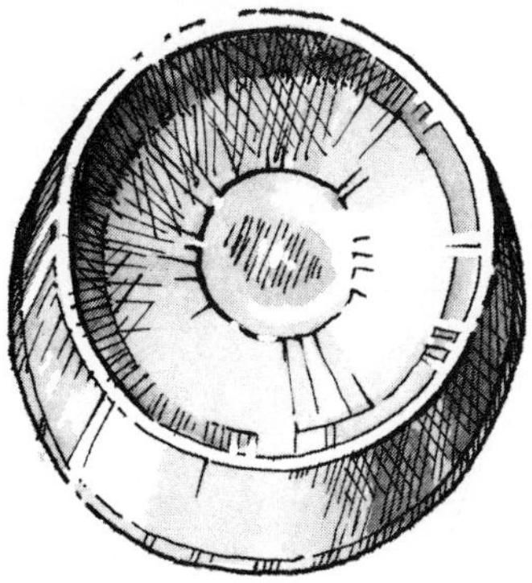

Figure 2-12 Food/water bowl, left

Figure 2-13 Gravity-flow food hopper, right

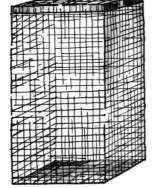

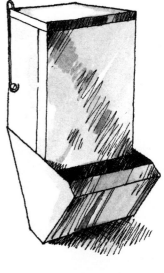

Figure 2-14 Wire-basket feeder, left

Figure 2-15 Chick feeder, right

Some animals will not accept food from a container, so it must be placed in the enclosure where they will find it. This creates some problems because any food not immediately eaten may decay and foul the cage. This is especially true of aquatic animals but it applies to other animals, such as snakes, toads, and salamanders. One way to resolve this problem is to place the animal in a separate container to feed it and then return it later to its home cage. This system works especially well for turtles. Otherwise, any uneaten food should be removed from the cage after the animal has had sufficient time to eat it.

Providing Water

Aquatic and semiaquatic animals will consume some of the water in which they live, and some animals obtain much of the water they need from their food. However, most animals should have fresh drinking water available at all times. For animals that will use them, the best way to provide water is with an inverted water bottle (Figure 2-16). Since the bottle is suspended

Figure 2-16 Inverted water bottle, left

Figure 2-17 Inverted vial, right

Figure 2-18 Water fountain

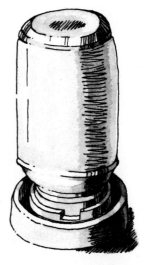

from the top or side of the cage, it takes up little space, is not easily spilled, and is not easily fouled by droppings or cage litter. It should be suspended as high as possible without being out of reach. If the cage litter comes in contact with the spout, the water will siphon out and flood the cage. However, when there are young animals in the cage, be sure to lower the bottle so that they can reach it.

An inverted vial (Figure 2-17), which is a modification of the inverted water bottle, is an excellent way to provide water for most insects. It is simply a pill vial or small jar filled with water and inverted on a few thicknesses of paper towel in a shallow dish or jar lid. The insects suck the water from the moist paper.

A water fountain (Figure 2-18) is also a modification of the inverted water bottle. It is used primarily for birds but can also be used for some large insect colonies if the bowl portion is filled with cotton so that the insects will not drown.

Some animals will only drink from an open water dish. When this is necessary, the dish should be heavy, like a food dish, or designed so that it does not easily tip. Many animals will soak for extended periods in the water, and it will often be fouled with wastes or substrate material. The bowl should therefore be rinsed and refilled daily.

Light Control

Animals, like humans, tend to function on a regular schedule that corresponds to day and night. During the week, normal classroom lighting will meet the needs of most animals. On weekends, light from a window should be sufficient. However, if an animal is kept in an interior room, it could be in darkness for as much as two and one-half days if the lights are out over weekends. Some animals might refuse to eat and drink during this time. This problem can easily be resolved by providing a light on a 12-hour timer or by moving the cage to a room with a window for the weekend.

Light is even more important if plants are kept in the cage or aquarium. In general, if the light requirements of the plants are met, the animal's needs will also be satisfied. However, a cage should never be placed in direct sunlight because the enclosed space can become extremely hot even though the surrounding temperature seems about right. To illuminate a cage artificially, use fluorescent lighting because it produces less heat.

Temperature Control

Temperature is an important consideration for all animals. Normal classroom temperatures are within the satisfactory range for most animals, even though ideal conditions may be slightly warmer or cooler. If the building temperature is reduced overnight or on weekends, special arrangements must be made. Many animals are susceptible to disease or lose their appetites when exposed to cold temperatures. And some will begin to prepare for hibernation when evening temperatures reach a certain low level. Hamsters, for example, will begin to prepare for hibernation when the temperature falls below 60° to 65° F (16°–18° C). In general, if the building temperature is reduced by 10° F (6° C) or more overnight or on weekends, a supplementary heat source should be considered. A standard submersible tank heater will maintain an appropriate temperature in an aquarium. Most cages can be warmed satisfactorily by positioning an incandescent light bulb (in a reflector) above them. However, careful monitoring with a thermometer is necessary when attempting to control the cage temperature with an external heat source.

Humidity Control

The amount of moisture in the air is probably the most overlooked environmental factor for captive animals. The air in a heated classroom is often very dry, sometimes as dry as a desert. Most animals are able to adjust to this situation, but others need special attention. The way an animal is housed will control the humidity to a great extent. A glass-covered planted terrarium, for example, will have a very high humidity level because both the plants and moist soil give off water and the cover prevents its escape. A screen-covered planted terrarium will have less humidity, and a sterile terrarium will have even less.

Sanitation

Other than a proper diet, there is probably nothing more important to an animal's well-being than sanitation. Most animals are usually quite clean; but all animals produce some wastes, and some do so prodigiously. In nature, wastes are usually eliminated in the animals' underground chambers or scattered as the animals go about their daily routines. These wastes disintegrate and rarely become a problem. In the confines of a cage, however, wastes can accumulate and not only cause potential health problems but also produce offensive odors. Therefore, it is important to clean the cage regularly. Other than complete negligence, probably nothing reflects a negative attitude toward animals more than allowing them to live in unsanitary conditions.

Activity Wheels

In nature, some animals occupy large areas and tend to be very active as they run from place to place to meet their daily needs. When confined to a cage, an animal has no real need to run, since all its needs are provided for. Yet some animals have a seemingly insatiable desire to run—it is a part of their normal behavior. One gerbil, for example, was recorded to have run on a monitored activity wheel for over two miles a night on several successive nights. In this regard, an activity wheel is not just a form of entertainment; it is an important environmental need. It simulates the home range that the animal would normally cover in its daily routine. Most activity wheels are designed to sit on the cage floor. However, a better alternative is to attach the wheel to the cage top or wall, so that it does not tip over or become clogged with litter.

Nest Boxes

Many animals will utilize a nest box for hiding, sleeping, and raising their young. But a nest box is more than a place to perform these functions. In nature, many animals, especially small mammals, have a nest in a burrow or a tree. Some burrows are extensive. Hamsters, for example, have deep tunnels with separate chambers for nesting and for storing food. Except for short forays above ground, they spend most of their time in these relatively secure places. Given a nest box, then, a hamster will not only sleep and hide there but will also use the box to store excess food.

Nest boxes for most animals can be constructed from standard one-inch unpainted lumber or plywood. Although less durable, sturdy cardboard boxes of appropriate sizes are satisfactory substitutes. An ample supply of nest material, such as cotton, undyed paper towels, clean soft cloths, or commercial nest material, should also be available. Some of this material can be placed in the nest box, but most animals that utilize nest boxes will carry the material inside if it is available in the cage.

Additional Environmental Factors

Most animals have rather specific environmental requirements and a fairly narrow tolerance to variation from the optimum. Yet, in nature, they have a surprising ability to adjust to a wide range of environmental conditions. Many of these adjustments are in the form of behavior. For example, if a basking lizard becomes too warm, it will change its position so that it absorbs less sunlight. Then, when it becomes cooler, it will return to its original position to warm up again. Similarly, a basking turtle will slide into the water when its body temperature reaches a certain level and then return to bask a while longer when it cools off. And a snake will coil up on a sun-heated rock to warm itself on a cool day. Many desert animals respond to hot midday temperatures by being more active at night or during the cooler twilight hours.

Some animals respond to, or even control, their ambient (surrounding) humidity through their habits and behavior, which makes it possible for them to survive in places where drinking water is limited. For example, when desert animals retire underground to avoid hot midday temperatures, they are also avoiding the dry desert air. The air in an underground burrow usually has a higher humidity level than the warmer surface air. When the animals come out at night, the cooler desert air is likely to have a higher relative humidity than it had during the day. Since animals tend to lose moisture in proportion to the humidity, being nocturnal keeps desert animals cooler and reduces their water loss.

Toads obtain most of their water by absorbing it through their skin, usually from moist soil. As the soil becomes drier, they bury themselves deeper to find more moisture. This is their normal daily routine—digging in during the day and coming out at night to search for food. During very dry periods, toads remain underground and will not surface until stimulated to do so by rainfall. In captivity, a toad will meet its water needs by soaking in its water container if the substrate is too dry.

There are many other ways that animals respond to environmental changes and stress through their behavior. But it is important to keep in mind that when confined to a cage, an animal often cannot respond as it would in nature. For this reason, it is very important that great care is taken to provide the animal with the most ideal environment possible.

Part 2   Invertebrates

The animal kingdom consists of a vast array of living things that range from microscopic organisms to 150-ton (135-t) blue whales that reach lengths of over 100 feet (30 m). One way to understand and appreciate this diversity is to divide the animals into groups with similar characteristics.

All animals that have backbones can be placed in one group, the *vertebrates,* so called because backbones are made up of individual bones called *vertebrae.* Vertebrates include fish, amphibians, reptiles, birds, and mammals. Conversely, animals that do not have backbones are called *invertebrates* ("without vertebrae"). The invertebrates include microscopic animals, sponges, jellyfish, worms, snails, clams, squids, starfish, insects, spiders, centipedes, millipedes, crayfish, and all of their close relatives.

Simplified View of the Animal Kingdom

Invertebrates

Protozoa
Sponges
Jellyfish
Worms
    Flatworms
    Roundworms
    Segmented Worms
Mollusks
    Clams
    Snails and Slugs
    Squids and Octopuses
    Chitons
    Tooth Shells
Echinoderms
    Sand Dollars, Sea Urchins, and Starfish
Arthropods
    Insects
    Spiders
    Crayfish, Crabs, and Lobsters
    Millipedes
    Centipedes

Vertebrates

Fish
Amphibians
Reptiles
Birds
Mammals

As a group, invertebrates are much more ancient than the vertebrates and are represented by some of the oldest fossils known. Fossil evidence indicates that invertebrates evolved from a few simple organisms living in the primitive seas to a diverse and complex group that sometimes reached high population levels. From the seas, they successfully invaded the land.

Primitive amphibians (the ancestors of frogs and toads) are sometimes wrongly credited with being the first land animals. More accurately, amphibians were the first land vertebrates. Long before the first amphibian wandered out of the sea, certain invertebrates had already done so, and with great success. In their new-found environment, terrestrial invertebrates became both diverse and abundant. In fact, one of the reasons given for the success of the amphibian land invasion was the abundance of terrestrial invertebrates for the amphibians to consume. Today, although often secretive and unnoticed, the invertebrates are still much more diverse and abundant than the vertebrates.

In the many years of their existence, invertebrates have adapted to almost every conceivable habitat. The oceans and seas where they originated still have a rich diversity of invertebrates. They are most abundant in warm, shallow coastal waters but may also be found in the depths of the open oceans and even in the polar seas. In all these areas, invertebrates are of great importance in many marine food chains. Some whales, for example, feed almost exclusively on small shrimp-like crustaceans. Throughout the millenniums, the secretions of some invertebrates have created great coral reefs; the shells of others have accumulated and, in some instances, been uplifted to produce major landforms.

Freshwater streams, lakes, and ponds also support a wide variety of invertebrates, including crayfish, snails, clams, many kinds of insects, and a host of microscopic organisms. Many of these invertebrates consume vegetation and decaying plant material. Because they are a primary source of food for fish and other animals, they are of great importance in aquatic food chains. Many terrestrial invertebrates, such as mosquitoes and other insects, spend the early stages of their lives in fresh water.

Terrestrial environments also host numerous invertebrates. To appreciate this diversity, one need only roll over a partially decayed log on a forest floor, exposing a variety of beetles and perhaps some centipedes, mil-

lipedes, crickets, ants, insect larvae, and earthworms. Moving a handful of nearby leaf litter would probably uncover other invertebrates, and a scoop of the underlying soil would include even more. Microscopic examination of the soil would not only reveal more kinds of invertebrates but would also show the extremely high levels of tiny insects and worms. And all of this is in just one tiny portion of only one environment. Considering all the possible environments and realizing that each has its own unique population, the total number of invertebrates is astounding.

Because of their diversity, it is difficult to generalize about the characteristics and habits of invertebrates, but their diversity is what makes them an exceptionally interesting group of animals to study. Many of them can be kept or raised in captivity; those described and discussed on the following pages were selected because of their popularity with children, their availability, their easy care, their unusual habits, or their usefulness as a source of food for other classroom animals.

Chapter 3 *Worms*

There are so many different kinds of worms in the world that it is difficult to make a single, accurate statement that describes them. Generally, worms are long, slender, soft-bodied animals that have no legs and therefore move by crawling. However, there are so many other animals that are wormlike in appearance, such as insect larvae and even some small snakes, that the word *worm* is often misapplied. Then, too, the animals that scientists call worms are so numerous and diverse that it is difficult to generalize about them. To simplify matters, scientists usually divide worms into three broad categories: flatworms, roundworms, and segmented worms.

Flatworms include two kinds of parasites—tapeworms and liver flukes—and one free-living type, the tiny planaria that live in freshwater streams and ponds. *Roundworms* are the most diverse of the worms and are, consequently, difficult to describe. To resolve this problem, some scientists have divided the roundworm group into smaller categories with more specific characteristics. But, generally, roundworms can be distinguished from other worms by being round (in cross section) and unsegmented. *Segmented worms* include earthworms and leeches. As the name implies, the body of a segmented worm is made up of individual segments placed end to end, which gives the body a characteristic ringed appearance.

Earthworms

Background

Earthworms—variously called angleworms, garden worms, redworms, fishing worms, and (when especially large) night crawlers—are found around the world wherever soil conditions are appropriate. There are many kinds of earthworms. Some are only 1 to 3 inches (2.5–7.6 cm) long when full grown, but one, a native of Australia, can reach a length of 3 yards (274 cm). Some kinds of earthworms are specific to a certain region or soil type, while others have a wide distribution. Except for size, there are few clues that distinguish one of the common types from another, but it is not necessary to classify an earthworm in order to study it.

Characteristics

Having no internal or external skeleton, earthworms are soft and fleshy. The long, cylindrical body consists of a series of rings called *segments*. The segments are progressively smaller toward the head end and, in some species, are somewhat flattened toward the tail end. An enlarged glandular area, the *clitellum*, partially surrounds the body about one fourth of the way between head and tail. Mucous glands keep the skin moist and give the worm a shiny appearance. Each segment has four pairs of tiny spines called *setae*—two pairs on the bottom and one on each side. The setae are too small to see but can be felt by holding the worm in one hand and gently sliding it through the fingers of the other.

All the important organs, including the brain, hearts (five pairs of them), reproductive structures, and stomach, are located in the region forward of the clitellum. The mouth is surrounded by the first ring, or segment, which forms the lips. The intestinal track, a straight tube, extends the length of the body, terminating at the last segment.

Many people mistakenly believe that an earthworm broken into two pieces will become two earthworms. It is true that, if the body is broken behind the clitellum and not too many segments are lost, the forward portion containing the internal organs will sometimes heal and survive. However, the rear portion, lacking these organs, will die.

Habits

As their name implies, earthworms spend most of their time burrowing in the soil. They burrow by two methods. If the soil is loose, they press their setae against the sides of the burrow to hold their position, then use their nose to push the particles of soil aside. They can also literally eat their way through the soil. Since earthworms need moisture, they will gradually burrow deeper if the topsoil becomes dry. And, as the soil cools in the autumn, they burrow down to spend the winter months below the frost line.

At night, especially when the soil is moist, earthworms come to the surface to consume organic debris and sometimes to mate. They usually extend only their forward portions out of the burrow; then, if disturbed, they can quickly withdraw to safety with a few rapid contractions of their muscular bodies. Sometimes, following an exceptionally heavy rainfall, earthworms come to the surface of the ground, apparently seeking drier areas. At these times, they can appear in large numbers on sidewalks and streets, where they sometimes become stranded.

Reproduction

Earthworms are *hermaphroditic*, that is, each one produces both sperm and egg cells. When two worms mate, each receives sperm from the other, then goes its separate way to complete the reproductive process. Later, the clitellum produces a mucous band that slips forward over the earthworm's body. Eggs and sperm are released into this band as it passes over the reproductive pores. As the band slips off the worm, each end closes to form an oval cocoon. The cocoon remains in the soil for two or three weeks before the eggs hatch. About three months later, the young worms will be fully grown.

Benefits to the Soil

Good soil and earthworms go together and even perpetuate each other. Earthworms prefer rich soil containing abundant organic material, which they consume for food. The organic material also helps keep the soil moist—a necessity for earthworms' survival. In turn, earthworms greatly improve the soil, first by releasing nutrients from the organic materials they consume, and, second, by mixing the soil and keeping it loose. Earthworm burrows also aerate the soil and increase its capacity to hold water. On the other hand, clay or sandy soils that contain little or no organic material and other types of soil that tend to dry out quickly often have low earthworm populations and, in their absence, rarely improve by natural means.

Earthworms are prolific, and in good soil conditions they can reach high population levels. Charles Darwin estimated that a single acre might contain as many as 50,000 earthworms. In general, the better the soil, the higher the earthworm population. However, many other animals, including birds, garter snakes, salamanders, toads, and a number of mammals, prey on earthworms. (And even though earthworms do not occur naturally in water, they sometimes become the prey of fish when offered on a hook.)

Earthworms in the Classroom

Earthworms are not as exciting as other classroom animals since they are often underground and rarely seen. However, a colony of earthworms can be useful as a source of natural food for other classroom animals, such as frogs, toads, salamanders, turtles, and garter snakes.

How to Obtain

An adequate supply of earthworms for classroom study can be found in almost any neighborhood by digging in a garden or overturning rocks, logs, or boards. Earthworms can also be found by searching a lawn with a flashlight the night after a soaking rain. Or they can be purchased from a bait shop or ordered from a biological supply company (see Resources, page 226).

Caring for Earthworms

Housing   Once obtained, earthworms can be kept in a variety of ways, depending on the teacher's plans. If they are to be held for only a few days, a dozen or two can be kept in a milk carton, cottage cheese container, or similar container half-filled with moist soil or sphagnum moss. A lid with small holes punched in it will prevent escapes and provide adequate ventilation. Earthworms should be kept cool to keep them inactive. (If they are placed in a refrigerator, they will live for several weeks.)

If the goal is to maintain a breeding earthworm colony, a larger and slightly more sophisticated system will be needed. In this case, the container should be as large as possible, because the greater the volume of soil, the easier it is to maintain a constant environment. A metal or plastic tub, for example, is sufficient to accommodate several hundred earthworms; proportionately fewer worms can be produced in a bucket or a standard aquarium. Good garden soil is a satisfactory medium, and if mixed with leaf litter, compost, peat, sawdust, or cow manure, it will be even better. Place 8 to 10 inches (20–25 cm) of the medium in the container, and add water as needed to keep the medium moist but not wet. Then two or three dozen earthworms can be placed on the surface and allowed to burrow into the soil. Placing a thin layer of leaf litter or shredded paper towels on the surface of the soil will help reduce moisture loss.

Earthworms in a cottage cheese container and a standard aquarium

Diet   If the soil is of good quality, the earthworms will not have to be fed for some time, but small amounts of food added to the surface will gradually disappear. Since earthworms will consume almost any type of organic debris, they can be fed shredded bits of grass, dried leaves, lettuce, and apple or potato peelings. Earthworms will also eat small amounts of soaked cornmeal, chicken mash, oatmeal, or coffee grounds. A little grass seed sprinkled on the soil will soon sprout and provide a natural food. The earthworms will eat the roots and, when the grass dies, they will also eat the leaves. If the system is watered enough to keep the grass healthy, the moisture level in the soil will be about right for the worms. Earthworms do not require light, so they can be kept in total darkness. (Even in the dark, grass seeds grown on the surface of the soil will sprout and grow for a while before being consumed by the worms.)

Earthworms will survive and reproduce at room temperature, but their optimum temperature is much lower — about 50°–60° F (10°–15° C). It is best, therefore, to keep the colony in the coolest part of the room.

When the Project Is Over

See page 10 in Chapter 1 for suggestions on what to do with animals that are no longer wanted or needed in the classroom.

Observations, Activities, and Questions

- Observe and describe an earthworm. Count the segments. Do all earthworms have the same number of segments?

- Place an earthworm on a moist paper towel and describe how it moves. Can an earthworm crawl backward? Gently touch it on the head, tail, and middle. How does it react in each case? Flash a bright light on the earthworm. How does it react?

- Moisten a finger with water and gently rub a large earthworm. Can you feel the setae?

- Place alternating 1-inch (2.5-cm) layers of moist sand and moist soil in a large transparent jar. Add a few earthworms and place the container in the dark (or cover it with black paper). Observe the layers at one week intervals, adding moisture if needed. What happens to the layers?

Chapter 4 *Mollusks*

The mollusks constitute a unique group of soft-bodied animals that differ in many ways from all other animals. At the same time, there are many kinds of mollusks and there is considerable diversity among them. The most common and, consequently, best-known mollusks are snails and clams. These groups are widespread throughout the world's marine and fresh waters. Some even live on land.

Another well-known group, whose members are less often seen because of their habits and secretive natures, includes squids and octopuses. Both of these mollusks live only in marine waters where the octopuses typically hide under rocks along the shoreline and the squids live in deeper, open waters. Two other groups of mollusks are the chitons and tooth shells. Both of these are marine, sedentary, and not often encountered. Tooth shells spend most of their time buried in the sand, and chitons remain attached to rocks along the shoreline.

Snails

Background

Snails, which belong to the ancient group of animals called *mollusks,* originated in the primordial sea, along with the octopus, squid, and the familiar clam. Some marine deposits contain snail fossils that are more than 500 million years old, and these fossils are some of the world's oldest with recognizable living descendants. Thus, the lowly snail, sometimes overlooked and best known for its "snail's pace," is distinguished (if it could speak for its ancestors) for having seen the origin of fish, the invasion of the land by amphibians, the rise and fall of the great dinosaurs, the conquest of the air by birds, and the dominance of the earth by mammals. During this time, snails became one of the most diverse and widespread of all animals and are surpassed only by the insects in their variety of living forms. One of their secrets of success is adaptability; snails can now be found in almost any permanent freshwater or marine environment, and some have also adapted to life on land.

Characteristics

Snails are easily recognized by their spiral shells. Since most snails withdraw into their shells for protection, the shell must grow as the snail grows. Thus, the shell is a spiral of increasing size. There are two styles of shells. In one, the spiral is in a flat plane like a coil of rope on the floor. However, since this kind of shell is cumbersome and difficult to transport, most snails have developed a more compact and easily carried shell with a cone-shaped spiral. But even this shell can be difficult to transport and maneuver among the leaf litter and vegetation of the forest floor. Some snail species have resolved this problem by developing a smaller shell, and, in some cases, the shell is so small that it no longer serves a protective function. A few snails have carried shell reduction to the extreme and have no shell at all. These snail-like mollusks without shells are called slugs. Some people think slugs are snails that have lost their shells, but this is true only in the evolutionary sense. For those snails that have a shell, it is a permanent, living, growing part of the body that cannot be abandoned.

The part of the snail that protrudes from the shell is called the foot, but it actually includes most of the animal's body. The flat-bottomed muscular part of the foot secretes a thin film of mucus, which provides lubrication, protects the soft body from abrasion, and helps the snail cling to rocks, twigs, and other surfaces as it glides along. The head, which is actually part of the foot, is equipped with tentacles—two pairs in most land snails and one pair in aquatic ones. One pair, always on top of the head, performs

Land snail

many of the snail's sensory functions. The second and smaller front pair, if present, is used for probing the surface ahead of the snail. The eyes are either at the base or on the tips of the tentacles on top of the head. The mouth is on the bottom of the head and contains a rasp-like tongue that is used to scrape off bits of food as the snail moves over surfaces like plants and rocks. Some of the snail's internal organs, such as the heart, kidneys, and intestines, remain inside the shell even when the snail's foot is fully extended.

Many aquatic snails obtain oxygen through gills, but this system is not satisfactory for terrestrial forms. Land snails take air into a breathing chamber through an opening, the breathing pore, on the right side of the body just below the shell. This opening can often be seen on land snails when the foot is fully extended from the shell. Some freshwater snails also have an air-breathing chamber, so they must occasionally come to the surface of the water for air or circulate oxygen-rich water through the opening.

Reproduction

There are several methods of reproduction in snails. Most terrestrial forms are *hermaphroditic,* that is, each snail has both male and female reproductive organs. When two of these snails mate, each receives sperm from the other. Then, each later produces eggs, which are laid among leaf litter, under a rock or log, or in some other hidden place where the eggs will stay moist until they hatch into tiny snails. Some aquatic snails are also hermaphroditic, but others are divided into males and females. In at least one species, all of the young start life as males, but some transform into females as they mature. Most aquatic snails deposit their eggs in a gelatin-like mass on some submerged object. One type of snail, however, does not lay eggs, but rather gives birth to live young.

Whatever their method of reproduction, snails are prolific and would reach high population levels if their numbers were not held in check by predators. Aquatic snails are consumed in great numbers by many species of birds, including herons and ducks. Turtles, fish, and certain mammals also consume large numbers of aquatic snails. Land snails are vulnerable to predation by birds and various small mammals, including rodents and shrews.

Most terrestrial and aquatic snails are primarily herbivores, feeding on a wide variety of vegetation including fungi and algae. However, they are opportunistic and will feed on the bodies of dead insects, earthworms, and, in the case of aquatic snails, dead fish.

Aquatic Snails in the Classroom

Aquatic snails are often kept in a classroom fish aquarium; but the fish usually receive most of the attention, while the snails are often overlooked or receive only superficial consideration. Keeping and studying snails as a separate classroom project, however, can provide an opportunity for students to focus their attention on one of the oldest, most diverse, and unique groups of animals on earth, the mollusks. And since aquatic snails are easy to obtain and care for, such a project can be conducted in the classroom with a minimum of equipment and expense.

How to Obtain

Aquatic snails are among the easiest animals to collect and keep in captivity. Almost any permanent body of water or permanently flowing stream will have a snail population. However, pond snails are easier to keep than stream snails because their habitat is simpler to duplicate in the classroom. Snails can be collected by searching through submerged vegetation or on the surface of any submerged object. The snails should be picked up gently as their shells are sometimes fragile and easily broken. Also, snails usually cling firmly to the substrate by their foot and will be injured if they are quickly pulled off. As soon as the snails are collected, they should be put in a container of the water from which they were taken. Enough water should also be collected to fill the container in which the snails will be kept. This will prevent the environmental shock that might occur if the snails were suddenly placed in water of a different quality. If possible, also collect a few pieces of the pond vegetation to decorate the snails' new home and provide them with a source of food.

If snail collecting is not practical, teachers can find aquatic snails and the plants needed for their habitat at local pet stores.

Caring for Aquatic Snails

Housing Aquatic snails can be kept in nearly any container that will hold water, but a transparent one will give students a good view of the snails, and one with a wide opening will allow for easy access. A 5- or 10-gallon aquarium is fine, but a quart or gallon wide-mouthed jar or transparent plastic container also makes a good snail aquarium. However, the snails should not be overcrowded—three to six per quart (or liter) of water (depending

Aquatic snails in an aquarium

on their size) is enough. The container can be set up like a typical freshwater aquarium. Put 1 to 2 inches (2.5–5 cm) of sand in the bottom to anchor the plants and provide a natural substrate. After adding pond water to within 3 to 4 inches (8–10 cm) of the top, gently push the plants into the sand, and add the snails. A loose-fitting cover will permit air exchange while minimizing evaporation. It will also prevent the snails from wandering out of the enclosure. To keep the plants healthy, place the aquarium where it will receive at least some indirect light each day.

Diet   Aquatic snails and their habitat are easy to maintain. The snails will eat small amounts of fish food if provided, but since they are primarily herbivores, they will obtain sufficient food by grazing on the aquatic vegetation.

The only regular maintenance needed is to replace the water as it gradually evaporates with fresh pond water or aged tap water—water that has been allowed to stand in an open container for 24 hours (see page 104). Otherwise, once established, aquatic snails can be maintained indefinitely throughout a school year with little effort.

Land Snails in the Classroom

Keeping land snails in the classroom, like studying aquatic snails, can provide the opportunity for students to experience a truly unique and interesting group of animals, the mollusks. And studying land snails in conjunction with aquatic snails can help students understand the important concept of animal adaptation to a specific environment.

How to Obtain

Although adapted to a terrestrial existence, land snails are susceptible to dehydration, so their activity is limited by the amount of available moisture. They tend to be most active at night when the humidity is higher and are most likely to be seen on the surface following a rainfall. Otherwise, they are usually found among leaf litter, under rocks or logs, or in other damp locations. During dry periods, land snails protect themselves by *estivating*, or withdrawing into the shell and sealing the opening with mucus until damp conditions recur.

Land snails are also available from some biological supply companies (see Resources, page 226) but usually not from local pet stores.

Caring for Land Snails

Housing   A wide-mouthed quart or gallon jar, a transparent plastic shoe box, or an aquarium that is arranged to simulate the natural environment is an ideal enclosure for land snails (and slugs). A cover is essential to maintain the necessary high humidity level and to keep the snails from escaping. However, some ventilation should also be provided, so the cover of the jar or shoe box should have holes punched in it. A few inches (centimeters) of moist soil will help maintain the humidity and provide a medium in which the snails can occasionally burrow and perhaps lay eggs. If the humidity becomes too low, the snails will begin to estivate. However, they can be encouraged to become active again by adding a little water to the soil.

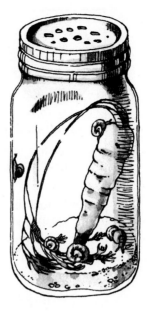

Land snails in a wide-mouthed jar
with a ventilated lid

Diet   Captive land snails will consume a variety of foods, but a diet of lettuce, carrots, apple, or celery will meet their needs and is easy to provide. An entire carrot can be placed in the terrarium and, although for their size snails can consume a surprising amount of food, this will last for several days. If provided with such a food source, snails can go unattended for weekends and vacations as long as they also have adequate moisture and are kept at an appropriate temperature.

When the Project Is Over

See page 10 in Chapter 1 for suggestions on what to do with animals that are no longer wanted or needed in the classroom.

Observations, Activities, and Questions

- Observe and describe a land snail or an aquatic snail. Find the shell, foot, head, tentacles, eyes, and breathing pore.

- Notice the bottom of a land or aquatic snail's foot when it crawls on the side of its container. How does it move? Can you see the mouth (try using a magnifier)? How does the snail eat?

- Using a magnifier, observe a cluster of aquatic snail eggs on a daily basis. Describe any changes that occur. How many individual eggs are there? How long does it take them to hatch?

- Flash a bright light on a land snail. How does it respond? Cast a shadow over a snail. How does it respond?

- Gently touch a land snail on one of its tentacles and then describe the snail's reaction.

Chapter 5   *Arthropods*

Arthropods are clearly the most abundant and diverse of the world's animals. In fact, this group is so large and diverse that it includes over 75 percent of the world's animal species. This diversity has allowed the arthropods to exploit virtually every conceivable habitat and food source on earth. But for all their diversity, all arthropods share three distinct characteristics: a firm external skeleton (called an *exoskeleton*), a segmented body, and several pairs of jointed legs.

The arthropods are divided into several familiar groups, called *classes*. The class Insecta, as the name implies, includes the insects. The class Arachnida includes scorpions, spiders, mites, and ticks. And the class Crustacea includes lobsters, shrimp, crabs, and crayfish. Other familiar but less well-known arthropod groups are the class Merostomata (horseshoe crabs), class Chilopoda (centipedes), and class Diplopoda (millipedes).

Crickets

Background

Of the several kinds of crickets that live in North America, the black field cricket is the most familiar. It lives in grassy fields, roadsides, vacant lots, gardens, and lawns. Another, the house cricket (sometimes called the gray cricket), is brown or gray in color and lives in similar places, but it is somewhat less common. Except for the difference in color and the house cricket's slightly longer wings, these two species are quite similar in appearance. A third kind, the cave or camel cricket (which is actually not a true cricket), resembles the other two but has a distinct hump on its back. The cave cricket favors cool, moist, dark places and is generally found under rocks and logs.

Crickets live in cracks in the ground, in small chambers that they dig in the soil, or under objects such as rocks or boards. Their food is mostly green plant material or some plant derivative, such as fruits or seeds. They need some moisture but usually obtain enough from their food. Because they prefer warm temperatures, they are most active during late summer and early fall; and, being primarily nocturnal, they are more often heard than seen.

The chirp of a cricket is an insect equivalent of a bird call: its primary purpose is to attract a mate or identify the cricket's territory. Only the males call, and the sound is made by rubbing the wings together (not the hind legs as is sometimes thought). The front wings have rough, rasplike surfaces that, when rubbed rapidly together, produce the chirping sound. Crickets perceive this sound, and others, with "ears" located on the inside of their front legs. (The ears consist of membranes that function like an eardrum to sense vibrations.)

Since the cricket is an *ectothermic*, or coldblooded, organism, its metabolism, and therefore its rate of calling, is affected by the ambient (surrounding) temperature. As a result, one can make a rough approximation of the temperature in degrees Fahrenheit by counting the number of chirps per 15 seconds and adding 40. To calculate the temperature in degrees Celsius, one would divide the number of chirps in one minute by 7 and add 4.

Characteristics

Crickets show the typical insect attributes. They have three body parts: head, thorax, and abdomen. The head is equipped with eyes and antennae for sensing the environment and a mouth. Two pairs of wings and three pairs of legs are attached to the thorax. The abdomen contains the reproductive organs and most of the digestive system. A row of small holes on the thorax and abdomen called *spiracles* are the openings to the respiratory system. All crickets have two projections about one-half the length of the body extending rearward from the abdomen. These projections are called *cerci* and are used to detect vibrations. Females have a third, longer, projection called the *ovipositor* between the cerci.

Reproduction

After mating, the female pushes her ovipositor into the soil and releases a single egg. This process may be repeated over 2,000 times in her brief lifetime. Crickets have gradual, or incomplete, *metamorphosis* (change in form). Each egg hatches into a tiny nymph, which only superficially resembles an adult. The nymph molts (sheds its exoskeleton) several times, each time becoming larger and more like an adult in appearance. With the final molt, the cricket becomes fully developed and sexually mature. The entire life cycle requires from two to four months depending on the temperature. Warmer temperatures speed the process.

Most adult crickets do not survive the winter, so the size of the summer population is largely a function of the eggs that overwinter in the soil. The population reaches its peak in the autumn as more and more crickets hatch. And, because the length of the average life cycle is temperature-dependent, the higher the average summer temperature, the higher the cricket population.

In nature, crickets are preyed upon by many animals, including birds, toads, and insect-eating snakes. Human beings have also learned to use crickets for a variety of purposes. In China and Japan, crickets are sometimes kept as house pets for the pleasure of hearing their song. They are excellent fish bait and food for pet lizards, toads, and larger aquarium fish. Crickets are also widely used in schools to study ecology, animal behavior, physiology, and entomology. House crickets are usually used for these purposes as they are easier to raise in captivity than field crickets.

Crickets in the Classroom

Crickets are easy to keep in the classroom—if one is prepared to tolerate a little chirping. Their needs are simple, and they can be kept in two ways, depending on the outcome desired. If the goal is to keep the crickets for a short time, a covered jar is satisfactory. A breeding colony, however, requires more space and a little additional care. In either case, field crickets or house crickets can be used, but house crickets are superior for rearing and breeding.

How to Obtain

Live crickets can either be collected from their environment or purchased from a local fish bait dealer or a pet shop. Or they can be ordered from a biological supply company (see Resources, page 226).

Caring for Crickets

Housing   To keep a cricket for a few days, place 1 to 2 inches (2.5–5 cm) of sand or soil in a jar with a ventilated cover. Add a dry leaf or a crumpled paper towel and the enclosure is complete. The soil will provide a medium in which the cricket can dig, and the leaf will give it a surface on which it can climb and a place to hide.

Cricket in a screen-covered jar

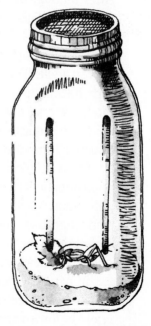

Diet   Crickets will eat a wide variety of foods, but a slice of apple, carrot, potato, or celery, or a piece of lettuce is a good short-term food as it will also provide the crickets with the moisture they need. The food should be replaced every day or two so that it will not decay or mold.

Assuming that they are given sufficient food and an appropriate environment, crickets can go unattended over weekends.

A Breeding Colony

A breeding colony of crickets can be kept in much the same way as a single cricket, except that a larger container is needed and two seemingly inconsistent requirements must be met. First, the environment must be kept dry to maintain the health and vigor of the colony. And, second, the crickets must have moist soil or sand in which to lay their eggs. Meeting these two requirements is the real secret to raising crickets.

A standard aquarium is an excellent container for housing a breeding colony. The crickets cannot climb the smooth glass walls, and the sides are tall enough to prevent them from jumping out—but a screen cover is recommended. Place 1 to 2 inches (2.5–5 cm) of dry sand or soil in the aquarium. Also add a shallow dish of moist sand or soil (a plastic margarine tub is perfect) for egg laying. The dish should be slightly recessed in the surrounding sand so that the crickets can climb into it. Crumpled paper towels will provide a hiding place and a surface for climbing, but empty egg cartons with a few holes punched in them are even better. If the cartons are put into the aquarium open side down, the crickets will climb inside and out.

Crickets will consume almost anything, including each other if they run out of food. Dry dog food is a well-balanced diet and is easy to provide, but crickets can also be well-nourished on oatmeal, cornflakes, bran, or any other grain cereal. Any dry food should, however, be supplemented occasionally with leafy or succulent vegetables. Water should be available continuously, but crickets will fall into an open container and drown. The best way to provide water is to invert a small jar or vial of water in a shallow dish with a few thicknesses of paper towel between the jar and the dish (see Figure 2-17 on page 22). The crickets will be able to get their water from the moist paper towels.

A small colony with 20 to 40 females can lay several hundred eggs each day. Adult crickets will eat some of the eggs (and will also cannibalize newly hatched young), so the dish should be removed after a few days and replaced with a fresh one if more eggs are to be collected. Put the dish with the eggs in another escape-proof container (a small aquarium or a plastic shoe box) for incubation and hatching. It is essential that the eggs do not dehydrate. This can be prevented by lightly sprinkling the soil with water as needed to keep it slightly moist. The eggs will hatch in three or four weeks at room temperature. (Cooler temperatures will prolong the hatching time.) The tiny nymphs will come to the surface of the soil and tumble out of the dish. At this time they can be fed, watered, and cared for just as the adults are. After about three weeks they can be kept with the adults with less risk of their being eaten.

Crickets will survive at room temperature, but they will be considerably more active and will reproduce better at higher temperatures — 80°–85° F (27°–29° C) is about right. A light bulb in the cage is a good heat source.

Keep the cage clean. Remove accumulated droppings, any dead crickets, and uneaten food. And remember, keep the colony dry.

When the Project Is Over

See page 10 in Chapter 1 for suggestions on what to do with animals that are no longer wanted or needed in the classroom.

Observations, Activities, and Questions

- Observe and describe a cricket. Find the three body parts. How many legs does the cricket have? How many antennae? How many abdominal projections? Is this cricket a male or a female?

- How does a cricket move? Jump? Walk?

- Observe and describe a cricket when it chirps. Do all crickets chirp?

- Try to determine the temperature by counting a cricket's chirps. For degrees Fahrenheit, count the number of chirps per 15 seconds and add 40. For degrees Celsius, divide the number of chirps in one minute by 7 and add 4.

- Observe and describe a cricket laying eggs.

- Observe and describe baby crickets. How do crickets change as they grow?

Praying Mantises

Background

Praying mantises rank among the most fascinating of North American insects. The combination of their large size, striking body form, and intriguing habits makes praying mantises especially interesting to keep and study in the classroom.

Many kinds of mantises are native to the tropics, but several also occur in North America. North American mantises tend to be either light brown or green—colors that allow them to blend with foliage and thus hide from their prey.

Characteristics

Like other insects, praying mantises have a body that is divided into three regions: the head, thorax, and abdomen. The head has a pair of large compound eyes and a pair of short antennae; the thorax provides the point of attachment for three pairs of legs and two pairs of wings; and the large abdomen contains most of the internal organs, including the circulatory, digestive, and reproductive systems.

A major difference between mantises and other insects is the structure of the thorax. In most insects the thorax consists of three short segments that are rigidly joined together, each segment supporting one pair of legs. In mantises, the forward thoracic segment is greatly elongated and is attached to the middle segment by a flexible, rather than a rigid, joint. This difference produces the feature that most people associate with mantises — a greatly elongated and flexible body, with the first pair of legs attached far forward and adapted for grasping and holding prey rather than for walking. The mantis's second and third thoracic segments still provide a firm base for the attachment of wings (yes, mantises can fly—although awkwardly) and two pairs of legs, which are the insect's primary means of walking and climbing. Another characteristic—and one that is shared with only a few other insects—is that mantises are able to move their head from side to side, a feature that is useful as they search for prey.

Praying mantises are named for the characteristic way they hold their forelegs. Because the forelegs are adapted for seizing prey rather than for locomotion, they are typically held in a folded position against the body when the insect is walking, flying, or sitting. This has been anthropomorphically described as *praying* (hence the mantis's name). However, since the forelegs thus folded are all set to reach out and grasp prey, the name *preying mantis* might be more appropriate.

Obtaining Food

Mantises seek their food either by slowly and quietly stalking through the vegetation or by lying in wait for passing prey. Their keen eyesight, flexible body, and ability to reach out quickly with their strong forelegs allow mantises to catch even flying prey. Mantises hold their catch securely with their forelegs and quickly consume it. Throughout their lives, mantises catch and consume a variety of insects and their larvae, spiders, and even other mantises. Often, however, only the soft parts are eaten, and wings, legs, and other hard parts are left behind.

Reproduction

After mating, which occurs in late summer or early fall, the female lays from 200 to 300 eggs in a frothy mass that is attached to some vegetation—often a weed or twig. The frothy material quickly hardens into a firm, somewhat oval, egg case, which resembles a piece of gray or tan foam insulation and is about one inch (2.5 cm) across. When the young mantises emerge from the egg cases in the spring, they are less than one-half inch (1 cm) long, wingless, and usually green. From the outset, they are voracious predators. As a result, they grow quickly. Growth is limited, however, by the *exoskeleton* (hard outer skin), so to increase in size, they must periodically molt (shed their skin). By late summer, they will be up to 3 inches (7.5 cm) long and, at the time of the final molt, will develop wings, become sexually mature, and mate to produce the eggs that will become the next year's mantis population.

After they mate, the females, continuing their predatory ways, sometimes consume their mates. One might look on this as the male's final contribution to the continuation of the species. But the females themselves don't live long after the laying of the eggs. Adult mantises do not overwinter, so, with the onset of cold weather, the female mantises—and any males that have lived beyond the mating process—die.

Mantises have a reputation for consuming other insects, so gardeners often welcome the presence of praying mantises. Sometimes they even buy mantis egg cases through garden catalogs in the hope that hungry young mantises will help reduce the insect population in a natural way. However, since the young gradually disperse from the place where they are hatched and many are lost to predators such as birds, the value of this practice is difficult to assess.

Praying Mantises in the Classroom

Because of their large size, interesting habits, and unusual method of capturing and consuming prey, praying mantises are one of the most fascinating insects to keep and study in the classroom. Their slow and deliberate movements are easy to observe, and their large size makes it easy for students to see and understand the intricacies of the insect body.

How to Obtain

Unfortunately, the natural population of mantises has declined in parts of their range—due perhaps to the use of pesticides and perhaps to the disappearance of the shrubs and other vegetation that are their natural haunts. And even where mantises are still numerous, their protective coloring and secretive nature make finding one a matter of luck. A good way to obtain adult mantises or egg cases for classroom study is to purchase them from a biological supply company (see Resources, page 226). As mentioned, egg cases can also be purchased through certain garden catalogs.

Caring for Praying Mantises

Housing   Housing needs vary slightly depending on whether one plans to keep an adult mantis or start with an egg case. An adult mantis can be kept in a large jar, a screen- or glass-covered terrarium, or even a wire cage. If the classroom stay will involve more than a few days or a weekend, the terrarium option should be selected. Since young mantises can crawl through a screen, a glass container with a cloth cover is needed if one plans to hatch an egg case. Whichever container is used, one or more twigs should be placed in the container to provide a surface for climbing and resting. And since mantises will prey on each other no matter how small (or large) they are, each mantis will need a separate container.

An egg case should be kept in a covered jar because the time of emergence cannot be determined. Both the developing eggs and the newly hatched young require a humid environment, which can be provided by placing some slightly moist soil in the bottom of the container. (Prevent egg cases from touching the moist soil by propping the twigs to which they are

Praying mantis in a
screen-covered terrarium

attached against the wall of the container. If an egg case is loose, attach it
to a twig or stem with a drop of white glue.)

As soon as the young emerge, they will begin to consume each other.
If left together, the entire reproductive effort of a pair of mantises may be
reduced to a single specimen in a short time. Therefore, it is best to decide
how many mantises you wish to keep and place them in separate containers. Release the remaining mantises in a suitable environment.

Diet   To feed newly hatched mantises, provide them with very tiny insects, such as fruit flies. The insects can be captured or raised (see page
70) and placed in the mantis cage. Or a young mantis can be placed in a fruit
fly culture, which will provide it with a source of food as long as the flies
reproduce.

An adult mantis can be fed any of its natural foods, which include almost
any kind of insect or insect larvae, such as crickets, grasshoppers, and flies.
Since mantises in nature capture their prey in vegetation, they might have
difficulty with ground-dwelling insects. If so, the food can be offered with
forceps. Some mantises will even learn to take food from your fingers. But
remember, mantises are predators, not scavengers; they must be given
live insects.

Captive mantises should be given water each day. Many will drink from
a drop on the end of a twig, and some will even take water from your finger.
A few drops can also be placed inside the cage near the mantis, and it will
drink the water as needed.

Weekend and vacation care can be easily provided if a mantis is kept in
a terrarium with a glass cover. If the soil is kept sufficiently moist, water
droplets will condense on the inside of the terrarium and on the plant
leaves. The mantis will consume these water droplets as needed, just as it
does in nature. Also, sufficient live insect food can be released in the terrarium so the mantis can feed at will.

**A Note
on Handling**

Praying mantises are secretive and difficult to find, but if you find one, it will be fairly easy to catch. If possible, maneuver the mantis into a jar or other container. A mantis can also be picked up but should be handled gently because it is fragile and can be easily injured. Also, mantises can and will bite, especially when they are first encountered. The bite is neither harmful nor painful, but the spines on the mantis's legs can inflict a painful wound.

**When the
Project Is Over**

See page 10 in Chapter 1 for suggestions on what to do with animals that are no longer wanted or needed in the classroom.

Observations, Activities, and Questions

- Observe and describe a praying mantis. Find the three body regions. How many legs does the mantis have? How many antennae? How is a praying mantis like (or different from) other insects?

- How does a praying mantis move? How does it use or hold each pair of legs?

- Feed a praying mantis and describe how it catches, holds, and eats its prey.

- Attach a thread to a small object about the size of a pea and dangle it at different distances in front of and to the side of a praying mantis. How does the mantis react? At what distance does the mantis seem to notice the object?

Walking Sticks

Background

Walking sticks occur both in the temperate and the tropical regions of the world. Some of the tropical species are notable for bizarre shapes and for colors resembling leaves or brilliant tropical flowers. Those that occur in North America are typical "stick insects" similar to the one pictured here. Their range is the United States and southern Canada east of the Rocky Mountains, and they are occasionally found in the southwest.

Although walking sticks are best known—and have been named—for their resemblance to twigs and sticks, these gentle insects have several other qualities that make them interesting to study and easy to keep in the classroom. Walking sticks' twiglike appearance is their major means of defense, and almost everything about them, from their shape and color to their habitat, diet, and behavior, is consistent with this mimicry. Few other organisms demonstrate so well the complementarity of structure, function, and behavior.

Characteristics

Walking sticks are related to crickets and grasshoppers, but, as seems evident from their appearance, they are even closer to mantises. Like other insects, walking sticks have three body parts—head, thorax, and abdomen—three pairs of legs, and a single pair of antennae. Most North American walking sticks are wingless. Thus, walking is their only means of locomotion. When first hatched, they are typically green in color, but as they mature, some gradually change to various shades of brown. Males are slightly more slender than the females and have a small pincerlike projection on the tip of their abdomen. And, as adults, walking sticks reach an impressive length of 3 to 4 inches (8–10 cm).

Camouflage

Walking sticks' camouflage, their principal line of defense, is of three types. *Protective resemblance* is the most obvious: a walking stick is shaped like a stick, with a head that is small and indistinct and a thorax and abdomen that are very long and slender. The illusion of twigginess is further enhanced by long, slender legs and antennae, which look like smaller branches on a twig. *Protective coloration*, another form of camouflage, complements the shape—walking sticks are either green or some shade of brown, the color of most twigs. The walking stick's *protective behavior* represents a third

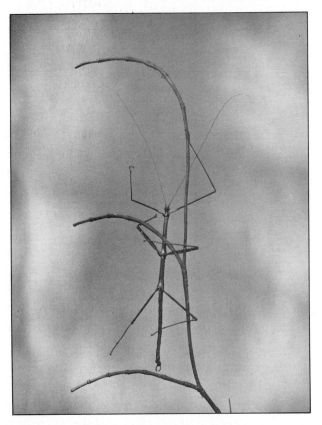

form of camouflage. The insects move slowly and deliberately and tend to "freeze" at the slightest disturbance, thus protecting themselves from predators and enhancing their resemblance to twigs. Some walking sticks, for whom camouflage may not be enough, also protect themselves by giving off a smelly chemical.

Habitat and Reproduction

Deciduous trees and shrubs provide the habitat, food and drink, and protection for walking sticks. The insects feed on leaves—seemingly preferring oak leaves, although they also eat those of maple, basswood, willow, and many other trees. Leaves also satisfy their needs for moisture. And, of course, the trees provide protection as well as a place to mate. Walking sticks mate and lay eggs in the autumn. Each female produces hundreds of tiny brown-and-white eggs, which are dropped from the trees and scattered over the forest floor. On the cool ground, walking stick eggs have a long incubation time, and most do not hatch until the spring following their second winter. Young "sticks," looking like tiny adults, then climb into the foliage, where they feed on the leaves, grow, and molt several times before becoming adults. Walking sticks do not survive the cold weather in places where freezing temperatures occur. For the most part, walking sticks, which do not bite or make noise, are innocuous as well as inconspicuous. Occasionally, when favorable conditions lead to an unusually large population, walking sticks are more in evidence and can even damage trees by defoliating them.

Walking Sticks in the Classroom

In addition to being fascinating to observe, walking sticks are masters of camouflage. Keeping and studying one or more walking sticks in the classroom can provide the opportunity for students to study the concepts of protective coloration, protective resemblance, and protective behavior. Furthermore, the walking sticks' large size and slow, deliberate movements make them easy to observe and study.

How to Obtain

A good method for collecting walking sticks is to search carefully through the foliage of trees or gently sweep the leaves with an insect net. Walking sticks are fragile — especially their legs, and they must be handled carefully to avoid harming them. The safest way is to encourage them to walk into a jar or into one hand by guiding them with the other hand.

Caring for Walking Sticks

Housing and Diet   Keep a single walking stick in a wide-mouthed jar with a ventilated lid and one or more walking sticks in a covered aquarium or screen-covered cage. A twig will give the walking stick a climbing and resting place. One or two fresh leaves, preferably from the tree where the walking stick was collected, will provide both food and water. Put about ½ inch (1 cm) of water in the bottom of the jar to keep the leaves fresh, especially over weekends. In a larger cage, a leafy twig in a vase of water will keep the residents in food and water for several days.

Walking stick in a screen-covered
wide-mouthed jar

To confine a walking stick outdoors, place a fine net bag (like some of
the laundry bags used for washing fragile items) over a twig with the walking stick and several leaves on it, and tie the opening around the twig. With
this technique, the only limitation to the time a walking stick can be kept is
the number of leaves in the enclosure. It is important, though, to place the
net cage where it will be shaded and where it will not be bothered by animals
or curious humans.

Hatching Eggs

A captive female will sometimes produce eggs. If so, they can be collected
for hatching and placed in a ventilated jar with 1½ to 2 inches (4–5 cm) of
slightly moist soil. Eggs kept at room temperature do not require the long
incubation period of eggs that remain outdoors and will hatch in 8 to 12
weeks—probably in the middle of winter when there will be no tree leaves
to feed the young—so it's a good idea to delay the hatching. This can be
done by keeping the eggs in a refrigerator until about February. Then the
young walking sticks will hatch at about the same time as the new leaves
appear, and they can be kept in the way already outlined for the adults.

When the Project Is Over

See page 10 in Chapter 1 for suggestions on what to do with animals that are
no longer wanted or needed in the classroom.

Observations, Activities, and Questions

- Observe and describe a walking stick. Find the three body parts. How many legs does the walking stick have? Does it have antennae? How is a walking stick like (or different from) other insects?

- Observe and describe how a walking stick moves.

- Observe and describe how a walking stick eats.

- Gently bump a walking stick's cage (or the twig it is resting on). How does the walking stick react? Why does it react this way?

- Discuss the various ways a walking stick avoids it enemies.

Mealworms

Background

Most insects, such as butterflies, moths, flies, and bees, are familiar to us in the adult stage of their life cycles. But the darkling beetle is best known in the larval stage, which we call the mealworm. Easily raised in large numbers, these golden-yellow grubs are used as fish bait, but they can also be very useful in the classroom either as a source of food for insect-eating classroom animals (such as toads, frogs, and salamanders) or as an interesting subject for classroom study.

Mealworms and darkling beetles, which are also called grain beetles or flour beetles, live where grain is grown, stored, or processed. Thus, barns, grain elevators, feed and flour mills, and warehouses for grain derivatives are typical places to find them. Unfortunately, they can also live in kitchen cabinets, where they might infest stored flour, oatmeal, cornmeal, or any other appropriate food source. Being secretive creatures, mealworms prefer relatively undisturbed places, such as the cracks, crevices, and corners where food is allowed to accumulate. A small amount of food will support several mealworms, and populations of hundreds or thousands can develop if sufficient food is available.

From Egg to Beetle

Darkling beetles have complete metamorphosis, so there are four distinct stages in their life cycle. The eggs, which are small, whitish, and difficult to find, hatch into larvae in one to two weeks. The larvae are very small when

63

first hatched from the tiny eggs but, except for their size, are similar in appearance to the larger mealworms. This is the longest stage of the life cycle, normally lasting four to six months, and is the only stage in which growth occurs. As they grow, the larvae molt several times, and with the

The darkling beetle in three of its stages: from left, larva (mealworm), pupa, adult

last molt the mealworms become pupae. Pupae are for the most part quiescent (inactive). But during this stage, which lasts from one to three weeks, major internal and external changes result in the development of the adult beetle. At first, the beetles are white and soft-bodied, but they harden quickly and change from white to reddish-brown and finally to black. Although the beetles typically live only about a month or more, the females begin laying eggs soon after transformation and may produce up to 500 eggs in this short time. The entire life cycle of the darkling beetle, then, lasts from five to seven months, with the temperature of the environment having a significant effect on the duration of each stage. Cooler temperatures will cause a longer period of development, while warmer temperatures will speed the process.

Mealworms in the Classroom

Mealworms are, for many reasons, ideal for classroom study. Their size and relatively slow movements make them easy for students to manipulate and they can be used in a variety of studies, including studies of insect life cycles and external anatomy. Also, since they can be raised in large numbers in a relatively small space, they make ideal food for classroom animals that require live insect food, such as frogs, toads, and anoles.

How to Obtain

You can usually obtain mealworms from a pet store or fish-bait dealer (ask for white worms or golden grubs). Mealworms can also be ordered from practically any biological supply company that deals in live animals (see Resources, page 226).

Caring for Mealworms

Housing   Mealworms can be housed in almost any container that will confine them and their food. A 5- or 10-gallon aquarium will house hundreds of mealworms; plastic ice cream containers, margarine tubs, or coffee cans are suitable for smaller colonies. Although the beetles have vestigial wings

Mealworms in a clear plastic sweater box

and cannot fly, a covered container will prevent any beetles from occasionally climbing out of the colony. The latter three containers come with snug-fitting plastic lids, which will need small air holes punched in them for ventilation. Plastic shoe or sweater storage boxes are ideal because they have loose-fitting lids that provide adequate ventilation, are a convenient size, and can be stacked to conserve space. The size of the container is also important since a colony's population seems to be more a function of how much surface area the beetles have than of how much food they have. Thus, a given amount of food divided among three or four plastic shoe boxes will produce many more mealworms than the same amount of food put in a single deeper container.

Diet   As mentioned earlier, mealworms can live on practically any type of dry grain derivative. They have been raised successfully in cornmeal, flour, oatmeal, cereal flakes of many kinds, and mixtures of these. However, bran or chick starter mash (available from a grain dealer or pet store) is better and will result in higher populations, more rapid growth, and more vigorous mealworm colonies.

Mealworms can complete the entire life cycle in a dry environment with no external source of water. To accomplish this, both the beetles and the larvae extract moisture from their food and conserve most of it by eliminating waste products as dry pellets. Occasionally, adults desire more moisture and obtain it by cannibalizing pupae or newly transformed adults if no other source of moisture is available. Mealworms will grow faster, and the adults will live longer and produce more eggs, if some small amount of moisture is provided. This is most easily accomplished by occasionally placing a slice of potato, carrot, or apple in the colony. A few drops of water can also be added, but the medium must not become wet. If it does (the smell of ammonia will be an obvious sign), the organisms should be transferred to a fresh medium.

A Breeding Colony

To establish a colony, put the mealworms in the desired container with 1 to 2 inches (2.5–5 cm) of food medium and cover the surface with a paper towel or two to provide a more secluded environment for the mealworms. At this point, the newly established culture should be left relatively undisturbed for a few weeks so that the mealworms can develop, pass through the pupal stage, and become egg-laying adults.

Once a culture containing all stages of the life cycle has been established, it will be self-perpetuating and will require little maintenance as long as additional food is occasionally added and moisture is provided as described above. About every three to six months, however, the culture should be rejuvenated by transferring all adults, pupae, and larvae to a fresh medium. Doing so eliminates accumulated droppings, dead organisms, and shed skins, and it stimulates faster reproduction. During this transfer, it is easy to subdivide the colony to make additional cultures. And if a little fresh medium is added to the old, a number of larvae will probably appear from eggs that were left behind when the colony was cleaned. Further, if the colony is rejuvenated in this way at the end of the school year and put in a closet or other dark place in the classroom, there should be an active colony at the beginning of the next school year.

When the Project Is Over

See page 10 in Chapter 1 for suggestions on what to do with animals that are no longer wanted or needed in the classroom.

Observations, Activities, and Questions

Establish minicultures for each student to observe by placing three to five mealworms in pill vials partially filled with appropriate food.

- Observe and describe a mealworm. Do all mealworms have the same number of legs? Body segments? Do they have eyes? Antennae? How do mealworms move?

- Carefully examine pupae and beetles. Do they have legs, wings, a head, and eyes? Do they have body segments? How are pupae and beetles like (or different from) mealworms?

- Find out if mealworms and beetles prefer to be in light or dark places. With light shining from above, shade part of the mealworms' container. Where do the mealworms congregate? Do the same with some beetles.

- Try to find out the preferred food of mealworms by placing different foods in each corner of a plastic box. Place eight to ten mealworms in the box and record how many worms are in each food every day for three or more days.

Fruit Flies

Background

Fruit flies—sometimes called vinegar flies, drosophila (after their scientific name *Drosophila melanogaster*), or, erroneously, gnats—are the diminutive insects that sometimes appear around fruit bowls or stored fruit. Since fruit flies are also attracted to fruit peelings and cores, they are often found around garbage cans and compost piles. And, of course, they are common in fruit-producing areas, where they feed and reproduce on overripe or decaying fruit. There are several kinds of fruit flies, all similar in appearance.

Characteristics

Although small—about ⅛ inch (4 mm) in length—and difficult to observe without a microscope or magnifier, fruit flies are similar to larger flies and show most of the typical insect attributes. They have three body parts: the head, thorax, and abdomen. The head has two prominent red eyes, a pair of barely perceptible antennae, and the mouth parts. Three pair of legs and a single pair of wings are attached to the thorax, which contains the heart and part of the digestive system (though most of the thorax is filled with muscles that move the wings and legs). The abdomen contains the remainder of the digestive system and the reproductive structures.

Fruit flies are generally yellowish in color with several black bands across the abdomen. Females and males can be readily distinguished by examining their abdomens with a magnifier. In male fruit flies, the tip of the abdomen is rounded and has a broad black band; in females, it is slightly more elongated and has a narrow black band. Also, the abdomen of the female has seven segments, while the male's has only five. These differences become more obvious when the female's abdomen becomes distended with eggs. Another distinguishing feature of the male (which requires still higher magnification to observe) is the "sex comb," several bristles found on each front leg.

Life Cycle and Reproduction

Fruit flies undergo complete metamorphosis, so there are four distinct stages in their life cycle: egg, larva, pupa, and adult. The length of the life cycle and of each stage is directly related to the temperature, with warmer temperatures tending to increase the rate of development. For example, at about 68° F (20° C), the entire life cycle takes about 15 days, but at 76° F (24° C), the time required is reduced to about 10 days.

Fruit flies produce astonishingly high numbers of offspring. A female fly, which can mate during the first day of her life and begin laying eggs the next day, can produce as many as 500 eggs in her first 10 days. She continues laying, though at a slower rate, for as long as one month. Under natural conditions, the fruit fly population is usually low following the rigors of winter, but as spring and summer progress, and as more fruit is available on which the flies can reproduce, their number continues to increase until a seasonal high is reached in the autumn.

Fruit flies can be annoying when they appear around a bowl of fruit, but most kinds of fruit flies are harmless. They do not have biting mouth parts, and they have not been implicated in the transmission of disease. And since they feed and reproduce primarily on decaying fruit, they do no harm to usable fruit. However, the Mediterranean fruit fly, which is not native to the United States, could pose a serious danger to crops. This species lays its eggs on unripened fruits, and the developing larvae (maggots) can destroy an entire crop before it can be harvested; but agriculture officials are taking great care to keep them under control.

Fruit flies are best known for their role in the study of heredity. Since they have a short life cycle, a high reproductive rate, and several easily identifiable characteristics, such as eye color and wing shape, it is possible to trace a single genetic trait through several generations in a relatively short time. As a result, fruit flies have probably contributed more to our knowledge of heredity than any other organism.

Fruit Flies in the Classroom

Since fruit flies are easy to raise in captivity, they are especially useful in teaching the concepts of metamorphosis and life cycle. They can also be used as food for anoles, web-spinning spiders, praying mantises, and other small insect-eating animals.

How to Obtain

Fruit flies are easy to raise in the classroom; so easy, in fact, that one autumn several generations of them lived and reproduced in a classroom jack-o-lantern (which was left in the room long after Halloween). This was discovered when someone bumped the jack-o-lantern and a cloud of flies emerged from the eyes, nose, and mouth. In this case, the flies lived there without any special care. Most teachers, though, will probably prefer to raise the flies under more controlled conditions and in enclosures.

Drosophila kits, available from some biological supply companies (see Resources, page 226), include everything that is needed — containers, media (food), and flies — in classroom quantities. However, the flies can also be cultured using readily available materials, and, as indicated by the jack-o-lantern experience described above, fruit flies are not hard to find — they will find you.

To trap wild fruit flies, put a few pieces of ripe, or even decaying, fruit — such as apple, cantaloupe, or banana — in open jars and place the jars outdoors. Placing the jars near refuse containers where the flies tend to congregate, while not necessary, will help ensure a good catch. It should take two or three weeks to establish the colonies. Flies hovering around the jars are a good sign that eggs have been laid inside, but even if no flies are visible, it is likely that some will have visited the traps and laid eggs on the fruit by this time. One need only place a cover (a piece of cloth secured with a rubber band) on the jars and bring them indoors. Keep the jars at room temperature, and the flies will reproduce and become the "stock" culture from which students can establish smaller colonies.

Caring for Fruit Flies

Housing   Students' fruit fly colonies can be housed in test tubes, plastic pill vials, baby food jars, or any similar containers. The size and shape of the containers is not important, but they do need covers that will both prevent the flies from escaping and allow air to enter. Cotton or foam rubber plugs will work in test tubes and small vials. Metal or plastic vial covers can be perforated with a paper punch or a nail and the holes can then be plugged with cotton.

Diet   Commercial fruit fly medium is probably the most convenient food source for fruit flies, but they can also be raised on various kinds of fruit, preferably very ripe or even partially decayed. The fruit should be cut or crushed so that the flies have access to the juices. In either case, place the fruit or medium in the small containers and add a loose wad of paper towel to hold it in place when the vial is tilted.

Transferring the Flies   Prepare to transfer flies from the stock culture to students' containers by sharply tapping the jar on the table to shake the flies to the bottom. Then quickly replace the cloth cover with a 3 x 5 inch card in which one or more holes have been made with a paper punch. If students invert their containers over the holes, the flies will crawl in. When 10

Fruit flies in a baby food jar and a
pill vial

or 12 flies have entered, students can quickly cover the containers and their cultures are complete.

Students should observe their colonies each day. The eggs, which the flies will lay on the cut surfaces of the fruit, will be difficult to see because they are so small. If students look carefully, they should be able to find some larvae after three or four days, but even these will be difficult to see at first as they are small and spend most of their time burrowing through and consuming the fruit. Eventually, after four or five days, the larvae will crawl out of the fruit and change into pupae. These, then, will soon change into adult flies, and the life cycle will have been completed within 10 to 15 days, depending on the temperature.

Through observing their fruit fly cultures, students can discover many things about insects and their life cycles. They may also be encouraged to use their ingenuity to find out about fruit fly food preferences and factors that affect reproduction and longevity.

When the Project Is Over

See page 10 in Chapter 1 for suggestions on what to do with animals that are no longer wanted or needed in the classroom.

Observations, Activities, and Questions

- Observe and describe each stage of the fruit fly life cycle—egg, larva, pupa, and adult. Which of them can move about? How do they move? How long does each stage last? During which stage does the most growth occur?

- Try to find out what foods fruit flies prefer by placing various fruits in jars and placing these outdoors. Wait two or three weeks and then see which foods have attracted more fruit flies.

- Find out whether fruit flies are affected by light. Shine a bright light on the fruit fly container. Do the fruit flies move toward or away from the light?

- Find out whether fruit flies are affected by gravity. Slowly rotate a container of flies. Which way do the flies appear to move?

Spiders

Background

Many people fear, dislike, misunderstand, and generally do not appreciate spiders. This is unfortunate because spiders, with all of their unique features and special adaptations, are exceptionally fascinating animals. It is true that some spiders have certain undesirable characteristics, but for the most part, their negative reputation is undeserved.

Spiders are among the most diverse and widespread of all animals. They can be found in almost every conceivable habitat, with the exception of the permanently frozen polar regions. Some spiders are even aquatic. And, as everyone knows, spiders are also adaptable and can thrive in, on, and around human dwellings. Most people are familiar with the common spiders found around houses and gardens, but many kinds are small, secretive, and rarely seen.

Characteristics

Spiders are arthropods and, as such, are related to insects and crustaceans. Like crustaceans, spiders have two major body regions: the *cephalothorax* (combined head and thorax) and the abdomen. (A thin waist, the *pedicel*, connects the cephalothorax with the abdomen.) But spiders are unique in many ways. Most of their internal features are attached to the cephalothorax. This includes the mouth, four pairs of legs, and, typically, eight eyes. A pair of leg-like structures, the *pedipalps*, is found between the front legs and the mouth. The pedipalps are usually small, but in tarantulas and a few other spiders, they are so large that they look like a fifth pair of legs. Internally, the cephalothorax contains the brain, a few nerves and blood vessels, and a portion of the digestive system; but most of the space is taken up by muscles that move the legs. The abdomen contains the heart, most of the complex digestive system, and a specialized gill called a *book lung*. The book lung gives spiders their high degree of adaptability to terrestrial environments. Gills must be kept moist in order to function, so most animals that have them must live in or near water, or at least in moist places. Since the gills of spiders are internal, they are protected from dehydration, which allows spiders to live in dry environments.

Producing and Using Silk

The ability to produce silk is not unique to spiders, but they have developed its production and use to a high degree. Silk is a protein fiber that is produced by special glands called *spinnerets* that are located in the abdomen of the spider. The silk of some spiders is exceptionally strong—even stronger that a piece of steel of the same diameter—and it can stretch to more than one fourth its length before breaking. Spiders use silk for many aspects of their lives, including catching and storing prey; constructing a home; making a covering for egg cases and, later, an enclosure for the young; running a safety line; and traveling from place to place.

Most spiders rarely fall because as they walk along, they occasionally touch their abdomen to the surface and attach a silk dragline. If they begin to fall or are brushed away, they are caught by the elastic silk line. Then they can either climb back up the line or produce more silk and lower themselves to a safe spot.

One of the more unusual uses of silk is for flight. Some small spiders use a technique called *ballooning* as a means of dispersing from their place of birth. The juvenile spiders climb some object, such as a rock, a post, or a tree, and begin releasing strands of silk into the air. When there is sufficient wind drag on the strands of silk to lift the small spiders, they release their grip and are carried away on the breeze. Using this technique, some spiders can be carried hundreds of miles (kilometers).

The best-known use of silk is in the construction of spider webs to capture prey. Spider webs are as diverse in structure as the spiders that weave them. Two of the more common types are the *orb web*, usually constructed in a vertical position across an open area, and the *funnel web*, with the apex

terminating in a crevice or other secret place where the spider hides. Spider webs have sticky fibers that entrap prey and nonsticky fibers that allow the spider to run over the surface without becoming entangled itself. In both types of webs, the spider sits quietly until an insect becomes caught in the sticky fibers. When the insect struggles to escape, vibrations in the web stimulate the spider to rush forward and seize the prey, which is then eaten immediately or encased in silk and stored for future use.

Capturing Prey

Most spiders are predators of insects and other arthropods, such as mites and even other spiders. They catch their prey in a variety of ways in addition to the use of webs. Some spiders stalk and jump on their prey. Tarantulas, wolf spiders, and some other large nocturnal spiders stand quietly until the prey bumps into the sensory hairs on their legs; then they simply seize the prey. In all these cases, the prey is immediately paralyzed by an injection from the spider's venomous fangs before being eaten or stored. Interestingly, since the prey is usually not killed but simply immobilized by the venom and since most small insects can live for a long time without eating, just a few stored insects can give spiders a good source of live food. With most spiders, eating is accomplished by injecting digestive juices into their prey and later sucking out the digested liquid food. Usually, the hard exoskeletons are not eaten, and these can often be seen on a spider's web.

Reproduction

Reproduction in spiders begins with courtship by the male. With orb spiders and other web-builders, the male finds the web of a female and plucks the threads with a characteristic rhythm to attract her attention. With other types of spiders, the male finds and follows the dragline of a female. With still other types, especially the jumping spider and spiders with good vision, visual cues such as dancing and leg-waving are used to attract the female. A few days after mating, the female lays her eggs and wraps them in a silk sac. In some species, the sac is hidden and the young emerge the following spring; in other species, the eggs hatch within a few weeks. In some species, the sac is carried by the female until the young hatch; and in some of these species, the young ride on the back of the female for a few days. After hatching, the young sometimes consume the silk sac. Then, following the pattern of the adult spiders, they become predators, with most living solitary lives.

About Spider Bites

Most spiders found in the United States and Canada do not bite, even when provoked. Of those that do, the bite typically causes only minor irritation that soon disappears. However, the bites of a few spiders, such as the brown recluse, can cause painful, slow-healing wounds. And the bite of the Black Widow, while not causing serious injury at the site of the bite, can result in severe internal pain and even death. Fortunately, very few people are bitten by either of these spiders and most survive, although with painful memories.

In fairness to spiders, it should be pointed out that the only mechanism they have for biting people is the fangs they use to inject enzymes into their prey, and the enzymes that paralyze and digest the prey are their only venoms. No spider is especially equipped to bite or poison human beings. The fact that some do is a coincidence of nature that allows their normal feeding mechanism to affect us in a negative way. The result, however, is the same. And since some spider bites are dangerous, all spiders should be handled with care—for example, by coaxing them into a jar rather than picking them up.

Spiders in the Classroom

Spiders are among the easiest of animals to keep and study in the classroom. The opportunity to do so can be an exciting learning experience for students and can help improve the image of one of the world's largest groups of animals.

How to Obtain

Since spiders are so widespread and abundant, they can be collected almost anywhere during the warm months. In natural areas, they may be found under rocks, logs, or pieces of bark. Also search for them (or their webs, which are the most visible clues to their presence) in gardens, in and around shrubbery, along foundations of buildings, and, of course, in basements.

Some kinds of spiders, especially tarantulas, can be purchased from pet stores or from biological supply companies (see Resources, page 226).

Caring for Spiders

Most kinds of spiders can be kept successfully in captivity. The method described below is satisfactory for maintaining most spiders. The needs of different spiders might vary slightly, but this can normally be determined by clues from the place where they are captured. Generally, spiders that live in very dry places will thrive in relatively dry conditions, but those that live near the water will require more moist conditions and perhaps a water dish.

Housing   A quart or gallon glass jar with a screen or hole-punched lid is an ideal container for most spiders. A terrarium is also suitable if it has an appropriate cover. In any case, because of their predatory habits, two spiders cannot be kept in the same container; one will consume the other. Place about 2 inches (5 cm) of moist soil in the container and then add a stick or two on which the spider can climb and attach its web. Spiders require some moisture, and they obtain it from their food and from the air. If the soil is sprinkled with water occasionally, the air will be kept appropriately moist for most spiders. Spiders that live in wet places should be provided with a small dish of water.

Spider in a screen-covered jar

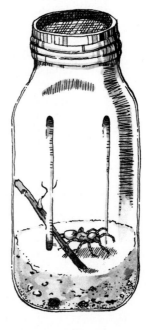

Diet   Spiders have the ability to survive for extended periods without eating, but they should not be forced to do so unnecessarily. It is difficult to generalize about the amount to feed spiders, so a little experimentation is needed. First, spiders can be fed a variety of insects, including flies, crickets, sowbugs, pill bugs, or even other spiders, but whatever food is used, it must be alive. Also, the food should be smaller than the spider being kept. Try feeding the spider once each week. If it eats each time, feed it a little more often. Of course, the frequency of feeding will depend on the size of the food. Most spiders can tolerate periods of cool temperatures, so no special attention is required for weekends and vacations.

When the Project Is Over

See page 10 in Chapter 1 for suggestions on what to do with animals that are no longer wanted or needed in the classroom.

Observations, Activities, and Questions

- Carefully observe and describe a spider. What is its shape? How many legs does it have? Does it have eyes? Does it have antennae?

- If two or more spiders are available, compare them. How are they alike? How are they different?

- Feed a spider and observe how it catches and consumes its prey.

- If a spider makes a web, look at it carefully and describe it. What is the shape of the web? What is the web attached to? How is it attached? Does the spider sit or climb on the web?

- If a spider sheds its skin, examine it carefully with a magnifier.

Daphnia

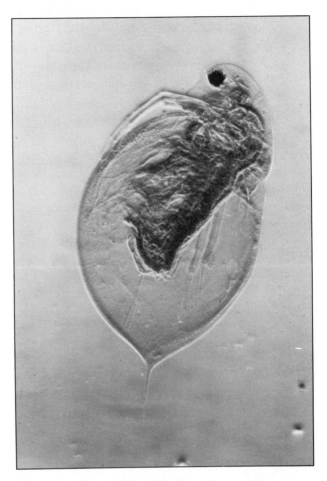

Background

Daphnia, often called water fleas, are diminutive aquatic organisms that inhabit freshwater environments throughout most of the temperate areas of North America. Their size, unusual features, and interesting habits make them intriguing to observe—and their role in aquatic food chains makes them valuable tools for teaching certain ecological principles. And because they are abundant in many areas and are easily collected and maintained, daphnia are excellent organisms for short-term classroom study.

Daphnia belong to the class Crustacea, a subgroup of the phylum Arthropoda (the largest group of animals on earth), which also includes insects and spiders. Also being relatives of shrimp, crayfish, and lobsters, daphnia are characterized by an external skeleton, numerous appendages, and gills.

Characteristics

Although they are complex organisms, daphnia are outwardly simplistic in structure. Superficially, they appear to consist only of an oval body (with no appendages) and a head with two prominent features—a single pair of antennae and a pair of eyes. In fact, daphnia have five or six pairs of legs and a short tail, but these are held close to the body and are covered from each side with a fold of the exoskeleton (the *carapace*), which obscures the legs and tail from view and gives the body a clamlike appearance.

The internal structures of the body—the circulatory, digestive, and reproductive systems—are visible through the light-tan exterior of the daphnia. Details of these structures, even the beating heart, can be observed with a low-power microscope or a magnifier.

Simplified daphnia anatomy

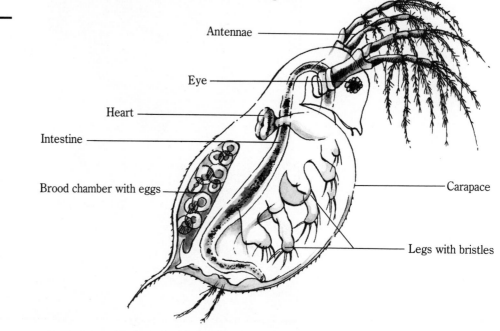

Antennae

Eye

Heart

Intestine

Brood chamber with eggs

Carapace

Legs with bristles

Locomotion

Daphnia are planktonic organisms, meaning that they are weak swimmers and tend to drift with the water's current. But daphnia are slightly heavier than water so that, without any active movement, they settle slowly toward the bottom. When drifting in this manner, the daphnia's antennae, which are held above the head, function like parachutes, keeping the tiny creatures upright. Then, by occasionally flipping their antennae rapidly downward, they propel themselves upward, in a jerky motion that makes them appear to be jumping. (This movement resembles that of terrestrial fleas, hence giving daphnia the name "water fleas.") Daphnia can control their vertical position in the water by either increasing or decreasing the rate of the antennae movement.

Habitat and Diet

Daphnia can be found in almost any type of freshwater habitat, including streams, lakes, ponds, swamps, and marshes (even those that become dry for periods of time). Interestingly, too, the daphnia's habitat to some extent determines their abundance. Larger lakes tend to have low but relatively stable populations throughout the year. In smaller lakes, ponds, marshes, and swamps, daphnia populations have wide annual fluctuations, with the highest levels occurring in late spring and again in late summer.

Daphnia feed on a wide variety of microscopic organisms, including algae, protozoa, bacteria, and decaying organic material suspended in the water. To gather food, daphnia generate a current of water with their legs, then filter out the suspended particles with a network of fine bristles on their legs. They then pass the concentrated food to the mouth and swallow.

Reproduction

The most intriguing features of daphnia are their methods of reproduction and how these methods are related to the prevailing environmental conditions. In normal, favorable conditions, a population of daphnia consists almost entirely of females, which reproduce generation after generation by *parthenogenesis* (without mating). Each female releases from 2 to 40 eggs into a brood chamber on her back. There the eggs soon hatch and the juveniles are released into the water where they quickly mature and begin to reproduce again parthenogenetically.

But should an environment become stressful—if the temperature cools dramatically or the food supply diminishes—each female's offspring will be made up of about half males and half females. These offspring will actually mate, and each of these females then produces highly resistant eggs that can tolerate harsh environmental conditions—even the drying-up of the water. Once the environment returns to favorable conditions, however, the resistant eggs hatch females that return to the parthenogenetic style of reproduction.

Daphnia are very prolific. Because each female is capable of producing broods of up to 40 offspring every two or three days for the month or more of her life, and because each new generation can reproduce within a few days, the population increases rapidly. In their abundance, then, daphnia are a major source of food for other aquatic organisms, especially fish. As a link between the microscopic food that daphnia consume and the larger predators that feed on them, daphnia have an important role in the energy flow of aquatic food chains.

Daphnia in the Classroom

Daphnia are especially interesting to keep and study in the classroom because of their unique form and unusual habits. Because they are so small and yet still just above the microscopic level, keeping and studying daphnia is a very useful way to introduce students to the abundant and unusual small aquatic life forms that are often unseen.

How to Obtain

During periods of high population, daphnia can be scooped up by the hundreds with a single sweep of a fine mesh aquarium dip net in a freshwater habitat. When the population is lower, several slow sweeps of the net through the water in a wide figure-eight motion might be required to accumulate a good many. Once captured, the tiny daphnia will stick to the moist net. To release them, simply turn the net inside out and lower it into a container of pond water into which the daphnia will swim away.

As you collect the daphnia, your catch will often include a number of other organisms, such as mosquito larvae and organic debris. To obtain a pure culture of daphnia, selectively recapture the daphnia from the first container by using a large-bore medicine dropper or a kitchen baster. Then transfer them to a second container of pond water. If at all possible, keep the daphnia in the water from which they were taken. To do so, collect several containers of the water at the same place you did the capturing. Pour the water through the collecting net into a second container to free it of any other organisms and debris.

Caring for Daphnia

Housing   Daphnia can live well in a gallon (or larger) glass or transparent plastic jar or a standard aquarium. But don't crowd them; a few dozen per gallon (4 L) is about right. And as they reproduce, be sure to divide the culture. If a supply of pond water is not available when dividing the culture, use aged tap water (see page 104), but do mix the tap water with water from the original culture to reduce the environmental shock that can occur when organisms are transferred to a very different environment. Daphnia can tolerate normal classroom temperatures, but they seem to do best below 70° F (21°C), so keep them in a cool part of the room, out of direct sunlight.

Diet   Daphnia do well on green water (algae), bacteria, or dry yeast. To produce green water for your daphnia, place a gallon jar of pond water under a bright artificial light or in a sunlit window. Single-celled algae, which occur naturally in the water, will reproduce profusely and soon turn the water green. Alternatively, start an algae culture by placing a teaspoon of garden soil in a gallon jar of tap water. Keep the jar in the light for a few days. As the green water is poured off, simply refill the container with water and add a drop or two of liquid fertilizer to provide a nutrient source, and the algae will continually regenerate.

Bacteria can be cultured by placing one half of a mashed boiled egg yolk in a quart (1 L) of water. Allow the mixture to stand at room temperature. After two or three days, the water will become cloudy, indicating a high bacteria population level. Yeast can be prepared for the daphnia culture by activating it in warm water (much as in baking).

To feed the daphnia, first siphon or pour out about one pint (.5 L) of water from the culture, to reduce the water level. Then add an equal amount of water from the algae, bacteria, or yeast culture. (This should turn the water slightly cloudy or green.) After two or three days, when the daphnia have cleared the water by consuming the food, simply repeat the process. This method of feeding the daphnia has the dual advantage of providing an adequate food supply and continually replacing some of the water, thus preventing buildup of waste products.

As an alternative, you might add a little mashed boiled egg yolk directly to the daphnia culture, where it will decay and produce bacteria for food. This method requires that you replace about one fourth of the water twice each week to remove accumulated waste material.

Kept as described, daphnia can sometimes be cultured continuously. However, some of the daphnia will eventually die (from age, if for no other reason). Dead daphnia will accumulate in the bottom of the container and should be left there. The dead specimens will decay and produce more bacteria on which the living daphnia will feed.

Because of the sometimes stressful conditions of their environment, captive daphnia may switch from parthenogenetic reproduction to producing resistant eggs. If this occurs, the population will gradually decline as the older daphnia die. But all is not lost. The accumulated debris will probably contain numerous resistant eggs, giving students an opportunity for further investigation. Just pour off as much water as possible (without losing the debris) and allow the debris to dry for several weeks. Then add fresh pond water or aged tap water. Though this is pure experimentation, and no results are guaranteed, it is possible that a new generation of parthenogenetic females will develop from the eggs.

When the Project Is Over

See page 10 in Chapter 1 for suggestions on what to do with animals that are no longer wanted or needed in the classroom.

Observations, Activities, and Questions

- Observe and describe a daphnia. (It might be helpful to isolate individual daphnia in vials or other small containers for each student. Magnifiers will also be useful.) Look for and describe the various body parts.

- Observe and describe how a daphnia moves.

- Find out whether daphnia are affected by light. To do so, shine a bright light on the culture from above and then from different sides. How do the daphnia respond?

Crayfish

Background

Over three hundred kinds of crayfish occur in North America. Each has specific habitat requirements and is thus limited in its range. However, since there are so many species, crayfish can be found in almost every imaginable aquatic or semiaquatic environment throughout most of southern Canada and the United States.

Crayfish—sometimes called crawfish, crawdads, mudbugs, or crabs— are freshwater organisms related to marine shrimp, crabs, and, of course, lobsters, which they closely resemble. All are members of a group called Crustacea, characterized by a hard exoskeleton, numerous legs, and the presence of gills. These, in turn, are members of a larger group, the Arthropoda, which includes insects and spiders and is the largest group of animals on earth.

Characteristics

Although they vary in length from 2 to 5 inches (5–12 cm) or more, most species of crayfish are so similar in appearance that it is difficult to distinguish among them. Usually reddish to brown or grey-brown in color, their bodies are divided into two parts: a rigid *cephalothorax* (combined head and thorax) and a flexible, segmented abdomen. Two pairs of antennae, a pair of eyes on stalks, and a mouth are located near the front of the cephalothorax, and five pairs of legs are attached to the midline along the bottom. The first pair of legs terminates in large pincers—the most obvious and characteristic feature of the crayfish. These are used in eating, jousting with other crayfish over territorial matters, defense, and burrowing. The four smaller pairs of legs are used primarily for walking but are also tipped with small claws. Most of the internal organs, including the brain, heart, lungs, and stomach, are in the cephalothorax. The abdomen looks and functions like a tail, but it, too, has small leglike appendages called *swimmerets* and a broad, flat, fanlike projection called a *telson*.

Walking is the chief method of locomotion for crayfish. Considering their cumbersome appearance, crayfish are surprisingly agile and can move forward, backward, or sideways in water or even on land, where they sometimes wander. Crayfish can also swim short distances, but they are awkward swimmers and adopt this way of getting around mostly as a means of escape. They swim by making a series of rapid downward and forward movements of the abdomen, which propels them backward in a jerking fashion.

Crayfish in an underground chamber just below the water table

Most crayfish live among rocks and litter on the bottom of streams, rivers, swamps, marshes, ponds, lakes, and muddy backwaters, and in these habitats they sometimes reach high population levels. Other, solitary, species burrow in fields and meadows, sometimes as deep as three feet (.9 m) to create underground chambers just below the water table. The entrances to these burrows are often "chimneys" of mud balls, the remains of the process of excavation. A few species called cave crayfish, unique because they are colorless and eyeless, inhabit underground streams sometimes hundreds of feet below the earth's surface.

Obtaining Food

Omnivorous and opportunistic in their feeding habits, crayfish play an important role in many aquatic ecosystems. First, as scavengers, they consume a great deal of dead plant and animal material that would otherwise decay. They also consume living plant material and, as predators, they eat insects and their larvae, worms, snails, fish, frog eggs, and tadpoles. When they eat, crayfish hold food against the mouth using one or both pincers, rasp away tiny bits, and then swallow.

In turn, crayfish are preyed on by many other animals, including various fish, turtles, snakes, minks, raccoons, and a number of birds, such as king-fishers and herons.

Reproduction

Reproduction in most species takes place in late summer or fall. A few weeks after mating, each female produces an average of 100 to 200 (but up to 400) dark-colored eggs. Once laid, the eggs are attached to the swimmerets and carried about by the female. When carrying the eggs, the female is said to be in the "berry stage."

After hatching, the young crayfish, which resemble miniature adults, remain attached to the swimmerets for one or two weeks. When they are about one-half inch (1 cm) in length, they leave the female and lead an independent existence.

Molting

The young crayfish grow rapidly and molt (shed their exoskeletons) several times before they reach maturity in as little as three to four months. Thereafter, both males and females molt two times each year — once to produce the breeding stage and once to produce the nonbreeding stage. Crayfish can regenerate an appendage that has been severely injured or broken off. The process begins with the next molt, and eventually a new leg or pincer appears.

For a few days following each molt, the new exoskeleton—including the greatest defense of the crayfish, the pincers—is soft and flexible. At this time, crayfish are especially vulnerable to predation, so they tend to be reclusive until the exoskeleton hardens. They are sometimes collected during this "softcraw" stage for use as fish bait.

A Delicacy

Considering their kinship to lobsters, shrimp, and crabs, it is not surprising that crayfish are edible. They are a well-known food in certain southern and West Coast states and are becoming increasingly popular in other parts of the country because they can be so easily raised on a commercial basis through aquaculture.

Crayfish in the Classroom

Crayfish are perhaps one of the most overlooked animals for use in the classroom. They are not only easy to obtain and maintain in the classroom, but they are also interesting to observe and nicely illustrate many aspects of animal behavior. Although they must be handled carefully to avoid the pincers, their size makes it very easy to observe the typical crustacean characteristics.

How to Obtain

Crayfish can often be collected from shallow streams. Place a large net downstream from a rock, and gently move the rock. This will alarm any crayfish sheltering under the rock, and as they attempt to escape, they will be swept into the net by the current. Crayfish can also be caught, with practice, by gently raising a rock and grabbing them. Or try fishing for them. Tie a string to a piece of meat or fish and dangle it near a crayfish. When the crayfish grasps the bait with its pincers, gently raise it out of the water and then lower it into a pail. No hook is needed as the crayfish will hold on and catch itself.

Crayfish are protected in some areas of the United States, so the propriety of collecting them, if in question, should be determined by contacting your state wildlife agency (see page 227 for the address). Crayfish can also often be purchased from fish-bait shops or from biological supply companies (see Resources, page 226).

Caring for Crayfish

Housing   Crayfish are highly territorial and will fight if crowded. This characteristic can be the source of interesting behavioral studies but it also needs to be considered in maintaining captive specimens. One or two crayfish can be kept in a standard aquarium. If more are kept, they should either

Crayfish in a standard aquarium

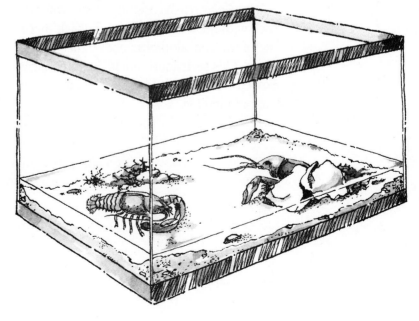

be given separate accommodations or placed in a larger container such as a plastic wading pool. One or two inches (2–5 cm) of coarse aquarium gravel will provide an appropriate substrate, and a few rocks, a brick, or a clay flower pot will provide essential climbing and hiding places. The addition of a few aquatic plants will make the enclosure look more natural and provide a continuous dietary supplement.

Crayfish have a seemingly uncontrollable urge to alter their surroundings. They will continually rearrange the substrate, and they often burrow under objects. Then they will defend the special area they have created from other crayfish. Crayfish need only 1 to 2 inches (2–5 cm) of water, but there should always be enough to completely cover the specimens.

Diet   Crayfish can be fed any of their natural foods. But, since these are sometimes unavailable and since crayfish are omnivores and scavengers, a variety of substitutes will also be acceptable. Small pieces of lettuce and other vegetables as well as pieces of fresh lean meat or fish will provide an adequate diet.

Crayfish are messy eaters, and it will be easier to keep their cage clean if they are removed to another container (a bowl or pail) for feeding. Otherwise, any uneaten food should be removed from the enclosure after half an hour or so to prevent fouling of the water. Since crayfish normally consume aquatic plants, they can be left over weekends and vacations without any additional attention.

A Note on Handling

Although crayfish can be taken out of the water for observation and study, their tolerance to dryness is limited since they breathe through gills. Consequently, they should not be kept out of the water for more than five to ten minutes at a time.

Handle crayfish carefully. They will not bite, but they can give a painful pinch with their strong claws. To pick them up safely, grasp them on either side of the cephalothorax above the walking legs with the thumb and forefinger. This technique should be demonstrated to students if they are to be allowed to handle crayfish. Alternatively, crayfish can be picked up with an aquarium dip net.

When the Project Is Over

See page 10 in Chapter 1 for suggestions on what to do with animals that are no longer wanted or needed in the classroom.

Observations, Activities, and Questions

- Observe and describe a crayfish. How many legs does it have? How many antennae? Are all the legs alike? Are all the antennae alike? How many body parts are there?

- How does a crayfish walk or swim?

- Observe and describe the use of the antennae, legs, and pincers in locating and consuming food, in defense, and in other activities.

- Save any shed exoskeletons and examine them with a magnifier. This will show details of the original crayfish—and will not pinch.

- Find out how crayfish interact with each other by placing two crayfish of different sizes in an established aquarium. Observe and describe their interactions and behavior. Which dominates the other? How does the submissive one behave? Remove the dominant crayfish and observe the reaction of the submissive one.

Land Hermit Crabs

Background

Hermit crabs are found in tropical and subtropical regions around the world. Most are marine and live their entire lives in the water. Land hermit crabs, however, live most of their lives on land, but they rarely wander more than a few hundred yards (meters) from some source of water. The land hermit crabs that are kept as pets are native to the shores of the Caribbean Islands and southern Florida.

Characteristics

Hermit crabs are crustaceans and are related to lobsters, crayfish, and, of course, other crabs, which they closely resemble. Like other members of this group, hermit crabs have two body regions: the *cephalothorax* (combined head and thorax) and the abdomen. The cephalothorax is covered with a hard exoskeleton, but the abdomen, which is protected by the shell, is soft and flexible. Most of the visible parts and internal organs are inside or attached to the cephalothorax. Hermit crabs have two pairs of antennae, which are used for sensing the environment; a pair of eyes, each on a movable stalk; and five pairs of legs. The first pair of legs has large pincers. One of the pincers, usually the one on the right, is larger than the other and is used for defense. The smaller pincers are used mostly for feeding. The next three pairs of legs each terminate in a sharp claw and are used for walking and climbing. The fifth pair, which is not visible from the outside, helps

90

the crab maneuver into and out of the shell. Other small appendages attached to the abdomen help the crab cling to the shell.

What appears to be one of the most obvious features of a hermit crab, the shell, is not part of the crab at all. It is only a borrowed piece of the environment to be later cast off and replaced. But the relationship between a hermit crab and its shell is an important one. The most obvious function of the shell is protection, which it provides very well. When a hermit crab withdraws into its shell, the large pincers cover the opening and protection is complete. A more interesting feature of the shell is related to breathing. All crabs breathe through gills, which must be kept moist. A land hermit crab carries a small amount of water in its shell, which keeps its gills moist and allows it to live in relatively dry environments. The shell is so important to a hermit crab that it rarely leaves it, and when it does, it is for only a very brief time.

Reproduction and Shell Exchange

Land hermit crabs return to the water to reproduce. The eggs hatch into tiny larvae, which go through several stages before developing into the familiar adults. It is only in the final stages that a young crab crawls out of the water and finds its first shell. At this time, the crab is quite small, so its shell must be fairly small, too, in order to be carried. The crab will eventually outgrow the shell and will have to exchange it for another. At this time, the crab will actively search for another shell of the proper dimensions, but not just any shell will do. The crab might examine several shells before selecting a new one. This examination involves probing the shell with the antennae, manipulating it with the legs, and even lifting it, apparently to determine its weight. Then, when everything seems satisfactory, the crab will carefully position the new shell and quickly exchange the old shell for the new one. If the new shell proves to be unsatisfactory, the crab will immediately move back to the original one.

Another type of shell exchange involves a trade between two hermit crabs. This is of special interest because it must involve some type of communication between them. In this case, two crabs, after a period of probing each other's shell, simultaneously leave their respective shells and enter the other. Sometimes this type of exchange involves several crabs exchanging at once.

As a hermit crab grows, it must periodically shed its hard exoskeleton. This is an especially vulnerable time for the crab because, in order to shed, it must leave the protection of the shell. Shedding, therefore, usually takes place in seclusion, under the cover of leaf litter or in some other hiding place. The entire process takes several hours. Shedding and shell exchange do not normally occur at the same time, so the larger crab, with its new exoskeleton, reenters the same shell. Then, if the original shell no longer meets its needs, the crab must search for another.

Although land hermit crabs can live out of the water, they are typically not found more than a few hundred yards (meters) from shore. They live on beaches and in and among the nearby vegetation, sometimes even climbing small trees and shrubs. They are primarily nocturnal and hide during the day, usually in the sand, under accumulated beach debris, or among leaf litter. At night they come out to feed on a wide variety of materials. They are omnivorous and will eat practically any plant or animal material that washes up on the beach.

Land Hermit Crabs in the Classroom

In many respects, land hermit crabs are one of the most interesting invertebrates for classroom study. Since they are fairly large and slow moving, they are easy to handle. Their environmental needs are simple, and since they eat almost anything, their food requirements are easy to meet. Even though their claws give them an ominous appearance, they are docile animals and do not often pinch.

How to Obtain

If one lives in southern Florida or on an island in the Caribbean, land hermit crabs can sometimes be collected from under debris or other objects within a few hundred yards (meters) of the shoreline. Otherwise, they can be purchased from some local pet stores, especially those that sell fish and aquarium supplies, or ordered from biological supply companies (see Resources, page 226).

Caring for Land Hermit Crabs

Housing   A standard 10-gallon aquarium is an ideal enclosure for land hermit crabs, and since they cannot jump or climb the sides, a cover is not necessary. Some sources recommend a moist sand or gravel substrate, but it is best to give them a dry environment. Crabs are messy eaters and bits of food dropped on the moist surface will quickly decay and foul the enclosure. An inch or two (2.5–5 cm) of dry sand, gravel, or even wood shavings

Land hermit crabs in a standard aquarium

makes a more suitable substrate. Water should be provided in a shallow dish recessed in the substrate to provide easy access. The crabs do not need to immerse themselves since they pick up the needed water with their claws. In fact, they may drown if the water is too deep. If the water dish is too deep or the sides too steep, place some rocks or gravel in the bottom to aid the crabs in crawling in and out. Also, since hermit crabs change shells as they grow, it is important to keep empty shells of varying sizes in the cage. This environment will meet the crabs' needs, but a rock and a stick or two propped against the side of the cage will add interest as the crabs climb them. Although there might occasionally be some interaction in the form of warnings and jousting, hermit crabs cannot harm each other, so several crabs can be housed together.

It is important to keep land hermit crabs warm. Normal classroom temperatures — about 70°F (21°C) — are about right for them, but being tropical creatures, they can tolerate even warmer temperatures. If the temperature gets below about 68°F (20°C), the crabs will become sluggish and inactive, and if the temperature drops below 50°F (10°C), they might die. If the classroom temperature is likely to drop significantly overnight or on weekends, the cage should be heated. This can easily be accomplished by suspending a 25–40 watt light bulb a few inches above the substrate as described in Chapter 2.

Diet As omnivores, land hermit crabs can be fed and kept healthy on a wide variety of commonly available foods. Fresh fruits, such as apples, bananas, and grapes, will be readily consumed. Hermit crabs will also accept meat scraps, fish, and canned or dry dog food. Simply place the food on the cage substrate, and the crabs will find it and eat as they wish. The crabs might not eat immediately, so the food should be left for a day or two and then removed. Sometimes it might appear that the crabs are not eating, but they do not eat much, and if food is available, they will eat what they need. Also, hermit crabs do not need to eat daily, so they can be left over weekends and vacations if their moisture and temperature needs are met.

A Note on Handling

When a hermit crab is first picked up, it usually withdraws into its shell for protection. After a few minutes, however, it will cautiously come out and resume its activity. Never attempt to force a hermit crab out of its shell. If the crab is pulled, its claws or legs may break off or, worse, the soft abdomen may be torn and the crab will die. A hermit crab will not give up its shell, even at the cost of its life. Care should also be taken not to drop the crab. A fall could easily break its legs or the shell.

When the Project Is Over

See page 10 in Chapter 1 for suggestions on what to do with animals that are no longer wanted or needed in the classroom.

Observations, Activities, and Questions

- Observe and describe a hermit crab. How many legs can be seen? Are all the legs alike? How many antennae are there?

- Watch a hermit crab when it is eating and walking. How does it use its legs and pincers?

- Observe the position of the claws when a hermit crab withdraws into its shell.

Part 3   Vertebrates

The vertebrates share a single feature that distinguishes them from all other animals—a backbone. Rather than being a single bone, as the name implies, a backbone is a column of individual cartilage or bone segments called *vertebrae*, the feature that gives this major division of the animal kingdom its name. This series of vertebrae forms a flexible, but strong, internal framework that runs the length of each animal's body and provides support for the head, other skeletal parts, and muscle attachments. However, there is considerable structural and functional diversity among animals with backbones, and these differences are used to divide the vertebrates into five distinct groups: fish, amphibians, reptiles, birds, and mammals.

As a group, the vertebrates are predated by millions of years in the geologic record by the invertebrates, but they are by no means new arrivals to the animal world. Scientists generally agree that the first fish appeared over 400 million years ago and, as the first vertebrate group, fish provided the stock from which all the other vertebrates developed. Since the appearance of the first fish, the world has gone through periods known as the Age of Fishes, the Age of Amphibians, the Age of Reptiles, the Age of Birds, and the Age of Mammals, as each of these animal groups experienced a period of development, rapid expansion, and subsequent decline. Although there are fewer kinds of vertebrates today than have lived throughout the millenniums, they are still diverse, widespread, and, perhaps, the most fascinating of all animals.

The characteristics of each vertebrate group are described in the following chapters, but the birds and mammals share a feature that is so unique that it deserves special consideration. Of all animals, only birds and mammals are capable of maintaining a consistent and relatively high body temperature—a phenomenon widely known as being warmblooded or *en-*

dothermic. Conversely, the body temperature of all other animals varies widely and is determined to a large extent by the surrounding temperature. These animals are called coldblooded or *ectothermic*. The significance of this lies in the fact that the rate of an animal's activity is directly related to its body temperature. Therefore, the activity level of a coldblooded animal is slower at lower temperatures and faster as the temperature increases. Thus, by being warmblooded, birds and mammals can maintain a constant rate of activity regardless of the external temperature. This means that they can run or fly as fast when the temperature is cold as when it is warm. They can catch their prey, avoid their enemies, and remain active all year rather than just during the warm seasons.

While being warmblooded has its advantages, there are also certain disadvantages. Or, looked at in another way, there are some advantages to being coldblooded. For example, the primary source of heat to maintain the consistently high body temperature of a warmblooded animal is the food it consumes. This means that warmblooded animals must have a fairly constant supply of high-energy food throughout the year and must therefore spend a great deal of their time hunting or grazing. On the other hand, since coldblooded animals obtain most of their heat from the environment, their food requirements are considerably less. They can live for extended periods of cool weather, even over winter, without feeding.

Collectively, there are over 20,000 kinds of vertebrate animals in the world, and they have many adaptations that allow them to live in a wide range of environments. Keeping and studying one or more of these animals in the classroom can help students know and understand the characteristics of the various vertebrate types and encourage them to appreciate the diversity and adaptations of the vertebrate groups.

Chapter 6 *Fish*

Fish are unique because they serve as the connecting link between the two major divisions of the animal kingdom. From some unknown invertebrate in the primordial seas, primitive fish evolved and became extremely diverse, even in ancient times. As the first vertebrate group, they flourished and provided the stock from which the amphibians developed. And from the amphibians came the reptiles, and from the reptiles came the birds and the mammals.

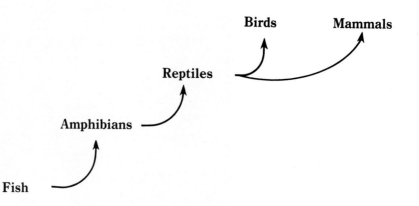

Diversity

The diversity in the kinds of fish that developed in primitive times continues today, partly because of the great variety of aquatic habitats and partly because fish have been able to adapt to the available habitats. There are two major groups of fish: those with skeletons of cartilage, which includes sharks and their relatives; and those with skeletons of bone, such as salmon, trout, and cod. Except for a few special cases, sharks live only in the oceans and seas, but bony fish can be found in both freshwater and saltwater habitats. The world's largest fish is a shark, the whale shark, which can be over 50 feet (15 m) long. The smallest fish is the goby, which is only one third of an inch (0.8 cm) long and is native to the jungle swamps of the Philippine Islands. Between these extremes, there are over 20,000 kinds of fish—more than all of the other vertebrate animals combined. Many of these fish are familiar, but some are unusual forms that are highly specialized for specific environments. One strange variety is a small, white, totally blind cave fish that lives only in underground streams. But probably the most bizarre of all are the fish with huge mouths, enormous teeth, and disproportionately small bodies that live in the ocean depths.

Environment

Water provides a unique environment for fish, and they are uniquely prepared to live in it. Most of what fish are and do is related to the characteristics of their watery environment. For example, water is a heavy medium, which means that it provides a great deal of buoyancy. Thus, by making only minor adjustments to the amount of air in their swim bladder, fish can remain suspended effortlessly at any level in the water. In this respect, they have essentially overcome the force of gravity and do not need limbs for support. The primary thrust for locomotion, then, is provided by rapid lateral (sideways) undulations of the body—not by fin movements as is often thought. Fish have two kinds of fins: paired fins, which are used for steering and guiding, and for slow forward and backward movements; and single fins, such as those on the back and tail, which provide stabilization as the fish swim. Finally, since water is a very dense medium and provides a great deal of resistance to movement, most fish, at least the fast-moving ones, are strongly streamlined, and scales help smooth out the body surface to reduce friction.

Fish are *ectothermic* (coldblooded), which means that their body temperature, and thus their metabolic rate, is directly controlled by the environmental temperature. This is often considered to be a disadvantage for terrestrial animals, since they must find ways to contend with wide daily and seasonal temperature fluctuations. However, water has a high specific heat. This means that the temperature of a body of water will not change rapidly. Even when the surface of a lake or pond freezes, the temperature at the bottom is usually several degrees above freezing. Thus, the aquatic environment is a very stable one in regard to both daily fluctuations and seasonal highs and lows; so, for fish, there is no great disadvantage to being ectothermic. Fish are most active during the warmer summer months when food is abundant; they are less active during the cooler months when food is less available. Yet they do not have to suffer the rigors of winter hibernation.

The amount of oxygen in water is never high compared with that in the atmosphere, and the level can vary considerably. Oxygen content is highest during the afternoon hours on bright, sunny summer days when aquatic vegetation is undergoing photosynthesis at a rapid rate. On the other hand, the oxygen level may be greatly reduced overnight as it is consumed by both plants and animals. Fish can tolerate the relatively low and fluctuating oxygen levels primarily because they breathe through gills, a highly efficient respiratory system. Interestingly, it is this respiratory efficiency, plus the fact that they are ectothermic and have reduced oxygen needs when cool, that allows fish to survive over winter in a frozen lake.

Fish sensory organs are similar to those of other vertebrates. Most fish have good vision, and, as suggested by the bright colors of some species, many have color vision. The sense of smell is especially acute in fish and, in fact, is the primary sense that is used in navigation for spawning. Pacific salmon, for example, use their sense of smell to return to the stream in which they were hatched to lay their own eggs after living in the ocean for several years. Fish do not have external ears, but they have a highly developed sense of hearing, which operates through a series of nerves and openings along the body. These are sometimes visible in the form of a lateral line. The sense of touch is also strongly developed, but fish probably have little if any sense of taste.

Reproduction

Methods of reproduction in fish vary, as one might expect from the great diversity of fish species. In one pattern, the female clears a nest in the bottom material and deposits the eggs; the male then swims over the nest, fertilizing the eggs by releasing *milt* (sperm) over them. Depending on the kind of fish, this might or might not be preceded by a mating ritual, and the nest might be guarded or simply abandoned. There are many variations to this pattern. In some, the eggs are attached to vegetation; in others, they are simply released into the water and settle to the bottom or drift with the current. In a few species, fertilization is internal, and the female gives birth to live young rather than laying eggs. Typically, fish do not provide parental care, but even this is a generalization, and there are a number of exceptions. Notable among these is the male mouth breeder, which collects and carries the young in his mouth for several weeks after they hatch.

Selecting Fish for the Classroom

Many fish species can be kept in the classroom. Determining which to keep depends on several factors. First, it should be noted that every state has laws protecting most native fish. Therefore, before collecting and keeping any native fish, consult your state's wildlife agency. (See page 227 for the agency's address.) Pet stores are a more typical source of aquarium fish, and they usually offer a wide selection, including both freshwater and marine species. While virtually all pet store fish can be kept under classroom conditions, some require sophisticated equipment, specialized food, and considerably more care than others. The salesperson might be able to make recommendations and answer any questions. However, unless you have experience in keeping fish, it is recommended that species that are noted for ease of care and hardiness be selected. Probably the easiest and most commonly kept aquarium fish are goldfish and guppies. Both are especially tolerant of classroom conditions and are recommended as first fish for the inexperienced aquarist.

Aquariums and the Aquatic Environment

An aquarium is simply a cage for aquatic animals. However, the aquatic environment is so drastically different from the terrestrial environment with which we are familiar that keeping an aquarium is often thought to be much more complicated than it really is. Aquariums can be kept with varying degrees of sophistication, but it is possible to keep quite simple versions in the classroom that are easy to maintain once they are established. An aquarium can be thought of as a small lake, and several questions about keeping an aquarium can be answered and understood by considering some natural lake processes.

Lake Processes

First, since water evaporates from the surface of a lake, its level would gradually decrease if the water were not replaced from two sources. Rainwater, which is relatively pure, falls in the lake, but this is normally not enough to replace the amount that is lost from evaporation. Rainwater also falls on the surrounding land, and this water, after dissolving some of the minerals from the soil, flows through streams to the lake. This is all monitored by the outlets, streams that flow out from the lake. If too much water enters, more flows out; if too little enters, less leaves. In the process, two things happen: the lake level remains fairly constant, and the lake is continually flushed, so the mineral and waste content of the water remains relatively constant.

Green plants living in the lake undergo *photosynthesis*. Utilizing sunlight as the energy source, the plants combine carbon dioxide and water to produce food—and in the process, give off oxygen, which is released into the water. Plants produce food for their own use. They obtain energy from the food by another process called *respiration*. In respiration, oxygen is combined with the food; in this process, energy, carbon dioxide, and a little water are produced. The energy is utilized by the plants, and the carbon dioxide and water are released into the lake. This is an interesting cycle. Plants take in carbon dioxide and water to produce food. Then, they utilize the food and give off carbon dioxide and water. Except for the fact that plants have gained food, it would appear that nothing has changed, but it has. An extremely important but often overlooked fact about this cycle is that the rate of photosynthesis is faster than the rate of respiration. This is logical, since a plant must produce its energy needs for a 24-hour period in something less than 12 hours of sunlight. So photosynthesis must be at least twice as fast as respiration. But a plant has to be even more efficient than this. If there were a cloudy day, or several cloudy days in succession, the plant would not have enough energy to survive through the night. So the plant always produces more food than it needs, just in case. It is this excess food and oxygen, and only the excess, that is available to animals. In a lake, then, the fish, snails, insects, and all other aquatic animals depend on the plants for their survival. As it turns out, plants can do nicely without animals, but the reverse is not true—animals cannot survive without plants to provide their food and oxygen.

Levels of Aquariums

Keeping fish successfully involves either duplicating or simulating these natural lake phenomena. This can be accomplished with varying degrees of sophistication, depending on the needs of the fish, the available equipment, and the time and interest of the keeper. For convenience, three levels of aquariums are discussed here.

Level One Aquarium   In its simplest form, the minimum aquarium arrangement that will meet the needs of fish consists of an appropriate container of water, some aquatic plants, and 1 to 2 inches (2.5–5 cm) of sand or gravel. The plants will provide both oxygen and hiding places for the fish, and the gravel will provide a rooting medium for the plants. Of course, some natural light will be necessary for the plants.

The water in the container will gradually evaporate, but more can be added to replace that which is lost. This simulates rainfall. About one third of the water should be changed once a month, simulating the outlet and natural flushing of a lake. The fish will have to be fed, and this simulates and supplements the production of food by plants. Although not necessary, a

Level One Aquarium

few snails will add interest and a more natural touch, since they are found in most aquatic environments. This simple arrangement is easy to maintain and will meet the needs of a few goldfish or guppies.

Level Two Aquarium   Even more sophisticated levels of aquaculture can be achieved through the use of additional equipment such as lights, filters, heaters, and aerators. Each of these simulates some aspect of the aquatic environment. Lights, for example, simulate the sun; a filter simulates the natural flushing of a lake; an aerator simulates the photosynthetic

Level Two Aquarium

addition of oxygen; and a heater simulates tropical temperatures and helps maintain a stable environment. The use of at least some of this equipment is necessary for keeping most tropical fish to ensure that their environmental needs are met.

Level Three Aquarium   A marine or saltwater aquarium is much more sophisticated and difficult to maintain than a freshwater aquarium. It requires most of the equipment described for a Level Two aquarium, as well as careful monitoring (chemical testing) of the water to ensure the proper salinity level. Although it is more difficult to maintain, the marine aquarium makes it possible to keep a wide variety of interesting organisms.

Although aquariums can be kept successfully in the classroom at all of the levels described, Level One is probably the most practical "first aquarium." It meets the minimum needs of some fish, is simple to establish and maintain, is interesting to observe, and provides worthwhile learning experiences for students. The sections on keeping goldfish and guppies that come later in this chapter will expand on the preparation and care of the Level One aquarium. Unless one has previous experience with fish, it is recommended that a more detailed book or an experienced aquarist be consulted before establishing a Level Two or Level Three aquarium. A pet shop employee may be a knowledgeable resource in this matter, too.

Some Commonly Asked Questions

How much should fish be fed?   The amount of food required depends on the type, size, and number of fish being kept, so some experimentation will be needed. In general, unless the fish selected have some special needs, they should be fed once a day with as much food as they will consume in five or ten minutes. Most fish will not overeat to the point of harming themselves, but it is still best not to overfeed them because uneaten food will foul the water.

How often should the water be changed?   Theoretically, the water in an aquarium should never have to be changed. However, if uneaten food is allowed to accumulate, bacterial action will cause it to decay. In the process, the bacteria will produce a foul odor, cause the water to become cloudy, and consume most or all of the oxygen. The foul odor and cloudy water are not in themselves harmful, but they indicate unfavorable conditions, and the reduced oxygen might kill the fish. Therefore, if the water becomes cloudy or smelly, it should be changed immediately. Otherwise, since there is no natural outlet, as in most lakes, it is a good idea to dip or siphon out about one third of the water once a month and replace it with aged tap water. This will reduce the accumulation of metabolic wastes and dissolve chemicals that are added when evaporated water is replaced.

What is aged tap water?   Tap water that has been allowed to sit in an open container at room temperature for 24 hours is called *aged tap water*. When water comes out of a faucet, it may contain a variety of chemicals, such as chlorine; or, in the case of well water, it may contain naturally occurring sulfur. These chemicals could have a detrimental effect on aquarium organisms. If the water is allowed to sit in an open container, most of the chemicals will dissipate into the atmosphere. Aging the water also allows the temperature to moderate. Any time water is added to an aquarium, aged tap water should be used.

Why does the water get cloudy?   If the water in an aquarium becomes cloudy, it is probably due to overfeeding, as mentioned above. However, if a fish or a plant dies and is not removed, it will decay and cloud the water, too.

What are the most important factors to consider in keeping an aquarium?   There are four basic factors to consider: (1) suitable water, (2) sufficient oxygen, (3) correct temperature, and (4) correct feeding of the fish. Each of these factors will vary with the kind of fish being kept. Understanding these factors and the needs of the specific fish will greatly enhance the pleasure of keeping an aquarium and help to ensure its success.

Should an aquarium be covered?   It is not necessary to cover an aquarium but doing so has some advantages. A cover will reduce the rate of evaporation, keep out dust, and keep the fish from jumping out of the aquarium. So, if a cover is available, it should be used. Otherwise, the first two problems are not major ones and the third can be resolved by keeping the water level at least 2 inches (5 cm) from the top.

Where should an aquarium be kept?   The most important consideration is the aquatic plants' need for light. But an aquarium should *not* be kept where it will receive direct sunlight. Direct sunlight can have several detrimental effects on an aquarium and its occupants. First, too much light will promote the growth of algae on the sides of the container, making frequent cleaning necessary. Also, most fish are adapted to living in shaded places, and some can actually be harmed by direct light. But most importantly, direct sunlight can cause the water temperature to become dangerously high and perhaps even kill the organisms. Otherwise, an aquarium can be kept any place where it will receive sufficient indirect light for the plants but not so much light as to cause other problems.

Goldfish

Background

Goldfish are native to the Orient and have been kept as captives for centuries in both China and Japan. From there they have been transported around the world and are probably the most popular of all captive fish. One of the reasons for their popularity is, no doubt, their striking coloration. In nature, though, they are brownish-gray to olive-green. The familiar gold and other variations in coloring are the result of centuries of selective breeding.

Another reason for their popularity is that goldfish are exceptionally hardy as compared with most other kinds of captive fish. Most of the small colorful aquarium fish are native to warm regions of the world and have thus become known as tropical fish. Tropical fish require a relatively warm and constant temperature. Goldfish, on the other hand, are native to temperate regions and can tolerate much more widely fluctuating temperatures. This makes it possible to keep them in outdoor pools and fountains as well as in indoor aquariums without special equipment to control the temperature.

Characteristics

Selective breeding has produced goldfish with a variety of body forms and colorations. The most common type has the typical streamlined shape. Another common variety has a double tail, a short dumpy body, an oversized head with protruding eyes, and elaborate fin development. Besides gold, goldfish can be white, orange, black, or any combination of these colors.

Because of their hardiness, escaped or released goldfish have become established in many places, where they usually revert back to their natural coloration and habits within a few generations. In nature, the habits of goldfish closely resemble those of their relative, the carp. They seem to prefer the shallow margins of lakes, ponds, and backwater areas. They consume a wide variety of foods, including vegetation, insects, insect larvae, crustaceans, snails, and worms. In searching for food, they often probe among the bottom material and, in the process, make the water muddy and disturb the nests of other fish.

Reproduction

At spawning time, which is usually in the spring, the female goldfish swims among thick aquatic vegetation and releases her eggs. The eggs are released either singly or in small clusters, but a total of 500 eggs can be released in a single spawning. The eggs usually adhere to plants and are fertilized by sperm released as the male pursues the female. Some eggs might be consumed in feeding, but otherwise they receive no further attention from the adults. At normal temperatures, the goldfish eggs hatch in three to five days.

The tiny *fry* (young fish) feed on microorganisms until they are large enough to consume the typical food of the adults. Their growth rate is variable and depends primarily on the available food and the water temperature. Maturity is usually reached when the fish become 3 to 4 inches (8–10 cm) long, but they sometimes grow to as much as 15 inches (38 cm) in length. They are long-lived, perhaps to 15 years or more, but usually stop reproducing by the ninth or tenth year.

Goldfish in the Classroom

Because they are hardy and easy to care for, goldfish are ideal first fish for the inexperienced aquarist and are excellent for the classroom aquarium. Since they are available in a variety of colors and forms, it is possible to maintain an interesting mixed aquarium without the additional equipment and care required for the more exotic tropical fish.

How to Obtain

Goldfish can be purchased from almost any pet shop that sells fish and aquarium supplies. They are also available in the pet centers of some discount and department stores and from some biological supply companies (see Resources, page 226).

Caring for Goldfish

Housing   A standard aquarium set up and maintained at Level One, as described on page 102, is a practical and suitable container for goldfish. The number of fish that can be kept is largely a function of their size. Normally, about one inch (2.5 cm) of fish (excluding the tial) can be kept for each gallon

(4 L) of water. In using this formula, figure the actual amount of water, not the volume of the container. Keep in mind that a portion of the space is taken up by gravel and that the water level does not reach the top. With this

Goldfish in a Level One aquarium

in mind, a 5-gallon (20-L) aquarium is suitable for 3 to 4 inches (8–10 cm) of goldfish, and a 10-gallon (40-L) aquarium can accommodate 6 to 8 inches (15–20 cm) of goldfish.

Diet   Commercial goldfish food will provide a satisfactory diet, but this can be supplemented with small amounts of natural foods, such as insect larvae and worms. Goldfish will also nibble at aquatic plants, and if snails are kept in the aquarium, the goldfish will probably consume some of the eggs and young snails. Goldfish do best when fed a small amount on a daily basis when it is convenient, but they can also be left without being fed over weekends and short vacations. In any case, they should be fed only what they will consume in a few minutes.

Breeding Goldfish

The conditions in an aquarium are not conducive to breeding goldfish. They might occasionally lay eggs, but in the confines of an aquarium, they are likely to find and consume all of the eggs or young. However, as noted earlier, goldfish can reproduce prodigiously if released in nature and may occasionally reproduce successfully in an outdoor fish pond. Conditions that favor reproduction in a fish pond include lots of vegetation where the eggs can be laid but not found and consumed.

When the Project Is Over

See page 10 in Chapter 1 for suggestions on what to do with animals that are no longer wanted or needed in the classroom.

Observations, Activities, and Questions

- Observe and describe a goldfish. How many fins does it have? How does it use the different fins when swimming forward? Backward? When turning?

- Observe and record the activities or movements of a goldfish in a five- or ten-minute period. Does it swim near the bottom of the aquarium? Does it swim near the surface? Does it investigate (nibble at) plants, snails, or other objects?

- How do two or more goldfish interact with each other?

- Gently place a new (inanimate) object, such as a colored marble, in the aquarium. How do the goldfish react to it? After the goldfish are familiar with it, place a similar object of a different color in the aquarium. How do the goldfish react to the new object? Can goldfish perceive color?

- Find out the breathing rate of a goldfish by counting the number of gill movements per minute.

Guppies

Background

Guppies are native to the northern parts of South America and the nearby Caribbean Islands. They live among the vegetation in freshwater marshes, swamps, and backwater areas of streams and rivers. They are primarily predators and feed on a wide variety of small aquatic organisms including mosquito larvae.

Characteristics

Those familiar with tropical fish might not recognize guppies collected from the wild. Although the females are typically larger than the males, wild guppies are generally smaller than the pet store varieties. Males are on average an inch (2.5 cm) long or slightly less. Females can be up to 1¼ inches (3 cm) long. Both the males and females are gray to grayish-green in color, and the males do not have the familiar elongated tails and bright colors characteristic of domestic guppies.

Guppies are among the most popular aquarium fish. Those available through pet stores are mutant strains or hybrids that have been selected for specific characteristics and now only superficially resemble their wild counterparts. There are two types of domestic guppies: common guppies and fancy guppies. Commons are usually smaller and less distinctively colored than fancies. However, in both types the male is typically smaller and more colorful and has a longer tail than the female. Through extensive cross-breeding, some female fancies have become quite large, sometimes as long as 2 inches (5 cm), and some have been induced to develop coloration, but they are still usually not as brightly colored as the males. Fancy males have been selected and bred to produce a variety of brilliant colors, including reds, blues, and yellows, as well as long flowing tails, which are sometimes as long as the bodies. Some of these males are among the most striking of freshwater aquarium fish.

Reproduction

Male guppies can usually be distinguished from females by their coloration and tail length, but they differ in one other important way. The anal (lower) fin of the males is modified into a long slender structure to guide sperm into the female during mating. This is of great significance because internal fertilization is rare in fish, and it allows the female to give birth to live young rather than laying eggs.

Reproduction in guppies begins with the male attempting to stimulate the female by "dancing" alongside and in front of her. This involves swimming slowly forward while rapidly vibrating the tail. If the female is receptive, the male moves into position beside her and, with a downward flip of the anal fin, quickly transfers the sperm. Following a single mating, a female can give birth to several broods at intervals of about four weeks. A brood might consist of up to 50 young or more, but 20 is more typical. The young mature in four to five months, so a single female and her offspring have the potential to produce an exceptionally large population in a relatively short period of time.

Both male and female guppies will consume some of their offspring. This is sometimes thought to be an active attempt on the part of the adults to limit population growth. However, this apparently deliberate cannibalism is really nothing more than a predator-prey relationship. Being predators, the adults simply do not distinguish between their tiny offspring and any other similar-sized prey.

Guppies in the Classroom

Guppies are excellent fish for a classroom aquarium. Compared with most other tropical fish, they are hardy, and the fact that they bear live young and will reproduce in captivity makes them especially interesting to study. They are also easy to care for and can be left for weekends and vacations without special care.

How to Obtain

Guppies are available from almost any pet store that sells fish and aquarium supplies. They can also be ordered from some biological supply companies (see Resources, page 226).

Caring for Guppies

Housing   A standard 5- or 10-gallon aquarium is suitable for several pairs of guppies. A single pair can also be kept on a long-term basis in a gallon jar. Since there is potential for overcrowding, it is good to limit the number of adults to one pair per gallon (4 L) of water. In either case, the aquarium should be maintained at least at Level One, as described on page 102. This is simply a container of water with 1 to 2 inches (2.5–5 cm) of sand or gravel and a few aquatic plants. The aquarium should be located where it will receive enough light for the plants, but direct sunlight should be avoided.

Guppies in a Level One gallon-jar aquarium

Guppies are more tolerant of temperature fluctuations than most other tropical fish. They can tolerate water temperatures of 65° to 85°F (18°–29°C), but temperatures of 70° to 75° (21°–24°C) are best. If the temperature is likely to get below 65°F (18°C) overnight or on weekends or if rapid fluctuations are expected, an aquarium heater should be used.

Diet   Dry commercial fish food will provide a satisfactory diet, but this can be supplemented occasionally with finely chopped fish or earthworms. Guppies will also actively consume tiny aquatic organisms, such as daphnia (collected from a marsh or swamp by sweeping an aquatic dip net through the water). Normally, guppies should be fed once each day, but only the amount they will consume in a few minutes. Although they can be left over weekends without being fed, some arrangements should be made to feed the guppies over vacations.

Breeding Guppies

If guppies are kept in a healthy environment, no special care is needed to encourage them to reproduce. Shortly after mating, the dark gravid spot on the female's abdomen becomes larger, due to stretching. By the time the female is ready to give birth, the gravid spot is quite large. The gestation period is about 28 days if the water temperature is 76°–78° F (24°–26° C), but it will be longer if the temperature is lower or allowed to fluctuate. Since adult guppies normally consume some of the young, the female can be placed in a "nursery" aquarium (a gallon jar) when she is about to give birth. Most of the young guppies will be saved if the nursery contains several pieces of vegetation for hiding places and if the female is soon returned to her home tank.

The young will not eat for a few days but will later feed on microscopic organisms that normally live in aquariums and are associated with the aquatic vegetation. After about a week, the young guppies can be fed the same food as the adults. The young can be kept in the nursery for three to four weeks, but as they grow, the litter should be divided and transferred to other aquariums or jars to prevent crowding. By this time, they can also be safely returned to the home tank without fear of their being consumed by the adults.

When the Project Is Over

See page 10 in Chapter 1 for suggestions on what to do with animals that are no longer wanted or needed in the classroom.

Observations, Activities, and Questions

- Observe and describe a male and a female guppy. How are they alike? How are they different? How many fins does each have? How do the fins on a male and a female guppy differ?

- If daphnia or some other tiny pond organisms are available, introduce a few into the guppy aquarium. How do the guppies react?

Chapter 7   *Amphibians*

Some three to four hundred million years ago, a fishlike organism learned to spend some of its time on land, starting a fad that really caught on. This was the first amphibian. No one knows why amphibians made the move to land. It has been suggested that amphibians, by spending time on land, were able to avoid the many predators in the water or that they were able to prey upon the many terrestrial insects. Some people have suggested that amphibians climbed onto land simply because "it was there." No one knows why the transition took place, but it was a fortuitous event. From this humble beginning, other amphibians evolved. And from these came the reptiles, and from the reptiles came the birds and the mammals. Although there once were several kinds and sizes of amphibians, they never reached the prominence and diversity attained by later vertebrates. Today, only two major groups of amphibians remain: those with tails, the salamanders; and those without tails, the frogs and toads.

Double Lives

Although most amphibians spend much of their time on land, they have, as a group, never completely given up their dependence on water. Most live in moist surroundings and return to the water to reproduce. The typical amphibian has three distinct stages in its life cycle. The egg and tadpole stages occur in the water, and the adult stage occurs on land. The transition from an aquatic to a terrestrial organism is a spectacular process that involves many anatomical changes and physiological adaptations. The eggs of frogs and toads are laid in water and soon hatch into tadpoles. The tadpoles feed on algae and decaying vegetation for two to three months, depending on the water temperature and the amount of available food, and then transform into adults. The first evidence of transformation is the appearance of the hind legs. Then the front legs appear, the mouth changes from a small oval to a wide slit, and the tail is absorbed. These external changes are accompanied by similarly spectacular internal changes as the tadpoles transform from aquatic herbivores to air-breathing, terrestrial insectivores. In a sense, every amphibian that makes this transition is retracing the steps of

Life Cycle of a Frog

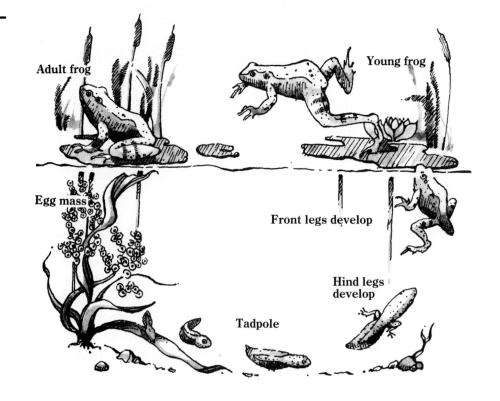

its primitive ancestors from water to land. Amphibians have never made a complete break from the water; because they live in two completely different environments, they are said to lead "double lives."

Much of what an amphibian is and does is related to the thwarted attempt to break away from the water. A frog's skin, for example, is thin and allows water to pass through. This permits the frog to "breathe through its skin" when it is under water but, at the same time, makes it vulnerable to dehydration when on land. To compensate, the frog has small glands that secrete an oily substance to keep its skin moist. Toads are more terrestrial than frogs and have carried the skin gland protective system to an extreme—thus giving them a warty appearance. The skin glands do not give amphibians complete protection from dehydration, however, so they further compensate through nocturnal behavior. Toads, for example, are primarily nocturnal and come out at night when there is more moisture in the air. During dry seasons, they bury themselves, digging deeper and deeper as the soil dries out. Through these various adaptations, some amphibians have the ability to live under remarkably dry conditions. However, all amphibians must find water to reproduce in, and this is a major factor in determining where amphibians can live.

Amphibians are found around the world wherever moisture and temperature permit. However, being *ectothermic* (coldblooded) limits their distribution. The diversity of species is greatest in tropical regions, where the temperature is ideal and does not fluctuate widely. In temperate regions, the diversity of species decreases, and the amphibians must hibernate in order to survive the colder months. Most species hibernate in the mud at the bottom of lakes, marshes, and streams.

Selecting Amphibians for the Classroom

Many small native amphibians, such as frogs, toads, and salamanders, can be kept successfully in the classroom. The most important factor to consider in their care is providing sufficient moisture to prevent dehydration. And, of course, accurate identification is necessary, since their needs vary from species to species. Some amphibians, especially toads, consume a relatively large amount of food, consisting of live organisms that may sometimes be difficult to provide in sufficient quantities. However, this problem can be largely alleviated by raising crickets, mealworms, or earthworms as a food source. (See pages 51, 66, and 35.)

Leopard Frogs

Background

Leopard frogs occur in appropriate habitats from southern Canada to Mexico and from the Atlantic coast westward almost to the Pacific Ocean. They are the most widespread and probably the best-known of all North American amphibians. As such, the leopard frog is likely to be the image that comes to most people's minds at the mention of the word *frog*.

Leopard frogs are reputed to be excellent fish bait and are collected and sold by the thousands for this purpose. They have also been widely used in research and for dissection and study in biology classes. And the muscular legs of larger leopard frogs are sometimes used for human consumption.

Characteristics

Leopard frogs are 2 to 4 inches (5–10 cm) long as adults. They may be various shades of brown or green and have numerous pea-sized black spots distributed irregularly over the back and sides. Their bellies and the undersides of their hind legs are white. Their amphibious nature is characterized by long, strong legs (which give them their well-known leaping ability on land or from land to water) and webbed toes (which make them powerful swimmers).

Habitats

The preferred habitats of leopard frogs include practically any type of fresh water, from weedy shorelines of large lakes to small marshes and streams.

However, leopard frogs also have a tendency to venture far from water, and this probably explains the other names by which they are known—*grass frogs* and *meadow frogs*. They usually sit quietly, camouflaged among the vegetation, waiting for prey. Because of their protective coloration and secretive habits, they frequently are not seen until they leap, often disappearing into the water or vegetation. However, they are stimulated to move about, especially at night, by warm summer rains. At these times, they often appear in large numbers, which no doubt gives rise to the folklore that it sometimes "rains frogs."

Reproduction

In the autumn, leopard frogs migrate to the bodies of water that will be their breeding pools the following spring. Entering the water, they bury themselves in the bottom mud, where they hibernate through the winter. When they emerge from hibernation, mating occurs; and the females produce hundreds of gelatin-covered eggs, which form a mass 3 to 5 inches (8–13 cm) in diameter. The eggs hatch in a few days into tadpoles, which feed on algae and decaying vegetation for two to three months and then go through the typical amphibian transformation into adulthood (see page 116). Newly transformed leopard frogs are usually 1½ to 2 inches (4–5 cm) in length.

Although leopard frogs are prolific and produce thousands of eggs, both the tadpoles and the adults are preyed upon, and their numbers have been held in balance by their many predators—fish, reptiles, birds, and mammals. Leopard frogs are protected somewhat from predators by their coloration, but leaping is their real means of defense. Several long, sporadic leaps through the vegetation not only help the frogs to escape but also confuse the predators.

Obtaining Food

The natural foods of leopard frogs—insects, spiders, caterpillars, and, occasionally, earthworms—are caught on the frog's moist tongue, then quickly drawn into the mouth and swallowed. Leopard frogs have especially good aim and can even catch flying insects.

Leopard Frogs in the Classroom

Leopard frogs are especially nice classroom animals for a variety of reasons. First, being widespread and usually abundant, they are easy to obtain. Once placed in an appropriate environment, they adjust nicely to classroom conditions and their care is easy to provide. They are also interesting to observe, especially at feeding time, and they can provide the focus for discussions of a variety of ecological concepts, such as predator and prey, adaptation, and camouflage.

How to Obtain

Leopard frogs can be captured wherever they occur in nature. Simply place one or both cupped hands over and then around the frog to confine it. But frogs have good vision and their primary means of escape is to leap, so you must move quickly to catch one. Leopard frogs can also be captured with a net. Otherwise, they can sometimes be obtained from fish-bait dealers or from biological supply companies (see Resources, page 226).

Caring for Leopard Frogs

Housing   Like many other amphibians, leopard frogs do not *drink* water. They have moist skin that permits the absorption and loss of water, and this must be considered when preparing an enclosure. They must always have a source of water in which they can soak; otherwise, they may quickly dehydrate. However, leopard frogs tend to eliminate wastes when they are soaking in the water and will absorb these wastes through their skin unless the water supply is kept clean.

Leopard frogs should be able to climb out of the water. Also, since the natural reaction of frogs is to leap when alarmed, they are likely to jump against the glass and injure themselves unless they are provided with a hiding place, such as a piece of log or a rock.

Leopard frog in a combination aquarium-terrarium

Considering all these factors, a planted terrarium, a modified terrarium with a water dish two inches (5 cm) deep, or a combination aquarium-terrarium will provide a practical, safe, healthy, and attractive environment for leopard frogs. Alternatively, a sterile terrarium with a gravel substrate can be used if water is provided and a piece of bark or wood is used to create a hiding place. Of course, whichever container is used, it should have a screen or glass cover to prevent escapes. (All of these enclosures are described and illustrated on pages 15–17.) Also, while leopard frogs do well at room temperature, they will thrive if the temperature is reduced overnight and on weekends.

Diet   Food in the form of live insects (such as crickets, darkling beetles, and ground beetles), mealworms, or earthworms can simply be placed in the cage near the frog. Leopard frogs will also learn to accept bits of lean meat loosely tied with a thread and dangled in front of them. Although it is best to feed them regularly, they can be left over weekends and short vacations without detrimental effects.

Health Captive leopard frogs seem to be more susceptible to disease than most other amphibians. They sometimes develop a disease known as red-leg. However, this is not likely to occur if the frogs are kept in an appropriate environment, if they have the opportunity to climb out of the water, if they have plenty of room (avoid crowding several frogs into the same enclosure), and if the water is kept clean.

A Note on Handling

Leopard frogs adjust well to captivity and are interesting to keep and study, but it is best not to handle them more than necessary. They never seem to adjust to being picked up and invariably attempt to escape, so they must be captured from their enclosure just as from outdoors—in cupped hands quickly placed over them. Once picked up, a leopard frog can be held in both cupped hands or in one hand with the thumb and index finger around the frog's neck and the other fingers firmly surrounding its body.

When the Project Is Over

See page 10 in Chapter 1 for suggestions on what to do with animals that are no longer wanted or needed in the classroom.

Observations, Activities, and Questions

- Observe and describe a leopard frog. Can you find the ears and nostrils? How many spots does the frog have? Do all leopard frogs have the same number of spots? How are the spots shaped? What color are the spots? How many toes are there on the front feet? How many toes are on the hind feet? Is there webbing between all of the toes?

- Describe how leopard frogs catch and swallow their prey.

- Place a leopard frog on the floor and measure how far it can leap.

- Determine the breathing rate of a leopard frog by counting the number of times its throat moves in one minute.

Tree Frogs

Background

There are several kinds of tree frogs in North America. Most of them are found only in the southeastern region of the United States, but the two most widely distributed kinds, the gray tree frog and the spring peeper, are found throughout the eastern half of the country and into southern Canada. Three other tree frog species occur in the southwestern states, and the range of one of these, the Pacific tree frog, extends northward along the west coast into Canada.

Characteristics

Tree frogs are relatively small compared with most other frogs. Depending on the species, full-grown adults are usually from ¾ to 2 inches (2–5 cm) in length. Although occasional specimens may be robust looking, tree frogs are generally slender-bodied and have long, slender legs. Their skin is slightly warty and, as a result, they are sometimes mistakenly called "tree toads." Tree frog coloration is typically green or brown, and some species have dark markings on the back. The single most distinguishing characteristic of tree frogs, however, is that each toe is tipped with a disk-shaped pad, which helps them cling to surfaces as they climb about.

The typical habitat of tree frogs is damp forests and woodlands. Being nocturnal, they spend the daylight hours either hidden among the leaf litter on the forest floor or sitting quietly on a limb or leaf. At night they climb silently through the trees and shrubs in search of their insect and spider prey. Because of their secretive habits and camouflage coloration, tree frogs are not often noticed by humans. They are occasionally seen, however, when their nocturnal search for food brings them to a window or a porch to catch insects that have been attracted to the light. Here, their climbing ability is aptly demonstrated as they scale the vertical glass surface in pursuit of insects. Otherwise, their presence can be detected when they call, sometimes persistently and in large numbers, from a spring breeding pool or, later in the summer, individually from an isolated perch in a tree.

Reproduction

The reproductive habits of tree frogs are similar to those of other frogs and toads. Soon after emerging from hibernation in the spring, male tree frogs enter shallow pools and begin calling. The females respond to the sound and enter the pools, where mating and egg laying occur. The adults then leave the water to live among the trees and shrubs for the remainder of the summer. The eggs soon hatch and the diminutive tadpoles feed on algae and decaying vegetation for several weeks before transforming into the adult stage. Thereafter, the young frogs leave the water to lead a life similar to that of the adults until the onset of autumn hibernation.

Tree Frogs in the Classroom

Tree frogs are among the easiest and most interesting of all amphibians to keep in captivity. They are docile and easily handled. Although they can jump short distances, they are primarily climbers and are not inclined to make the surprising and sporadic leaps characteristic of other frogs. They will sit quietly for hours; yet they are alert and become active predators when presented with their live insect food. Once provided with an appropriate enclosure and food, tree frogs require little attention and care.

How to Obtain

In the spring, when they are calling from the edge of their breeding pools, tree frogs can easily be located at night with a flashlight and picked up by hand. During the summer and early autumn, they can be captured when they appear around a light source to capture insects. Otherwise, they are difficult to find among the foliage where they normally occur because they are so secretive and well camouflaged.

Caring for Tree Frogs

Housing   A planted terrarium, especially one that simulates the tree frog's natural habitat, is an excellent environment for a tree frog if the plants are given appropriate care in the form of light, temperature, and water. The plants make good climbing and hiding places, and the moisture in the soil and that given off by the plants will help maintain an adequate level of humidity. A little moss, a few dried leaves, and perhaps a rock, a piece of bark, and a stick or two will give a more natural appearance and add additional climbing and hiding places. Of course, a cover is necessary to prevent the frogs from escaping. While a screen cover is sufficient, a glass one is preferable as it will help maintain the high humidity that is important to both the frog and the plants.

Tree frogs in a planted terrarium

A convenient alternative to a planted terrarium, and one that has most of its advantages, is a modified terrarium, which can be created by placing a potted plant in a closed container large enough to accommodate it. An even less sophisticated arrangement—but a satisfactory one on a short-term basis—can be provided by simply placing a few moist paper towels in the bottom of the container and adding a stick or two for climbing. Since tree frogs are relatively inactive, the size of the enclosure is not especially important as long as it is not too confining. A standard aquarium is more than adequate, and a plastic sweater box or a gallon jar is sufficient if a proper environment is established.

Whatever the arrangement, remember that tree frogs, like most other amphibians, are susceptible to dehydration. Maintaining a high humidity level in the cage is necessary for their comfort and survival. Moist soil and plants will help provide the necessary moisture level. And even though tree frogs rarely, if ever, drink, they should always be provided with a container of clean water in which they can soak to maintain their water balance.

Diet   The normal food of tree frogs is live insects and spiders, which they catch in their arboreal environment. In captivity, they should be provided with a similar diet. A sufficient quantity of insects can usually be collected at night around a lighted window or during the day under rocks and boards. Alternatively, tree frogs can be fed mealworms or crickets that have been raised in the classroom (see pages 66 and 51) or purchased from a local pet store. As with most other amphibians, the food must be alive because it is movement that stimulates the tree frog's feeding reaction. It is surprising how large an object these frogs can consume in proportion to their own size, but they seem to prefer food that is approximately one-fourth to one-third their own length.

In nature, tree frogs are opportunistic feeders and will consume what they can when it is available. Then, if necessary, they might go for a day or two without eating. This natural feeding cycle makes it possible to keep a tree frog over weekends and short vacations without special care. However, a few live insects left in the frog's enclosure will allow the tree frog to eat if it chooses to do so.

A Note on Handling

Because of their small size and docile nature, tree frogs can easily be picked up and held in one or both cupped hands. A tree frog might even sit quietly on one's hand for a while. Eventually, however, it will leap and perhaps escape or hurt itself, so it should always be covered when in hand. Since a tree frog cannot be observed in this way, it is best to leave it in its enclosure where it can be more easily seen.

When the Project Is Over

See page 10 in Chapter 1 for suggestions on what to do with animals that are no longer wanted or needed in the classroom.

Observations, Activities, and Questions

- Observe and describe a tree frog. Can you find the ears and nostrils? How many toes does a tree frog have on the front feet? How many toes are on the hind feet? Describe the toes.

- Describe how a tree frog catches and swallows its prey.

- Place a tree frog on the floor and describe how it moves.

- Determine the breathing rate of a tree frog by counting the number of times its throat moves in one minute.

Toads

Background

There are three kinds of toads in North America. The spadefoot toads, found in various places east of the Rocky Mountains and a few areas of the southwestern states, are smooth skinned, secretive, and rarely seen. The narrow-mouthed toads of the southern states are also smooth skinned and small as compared with other toads. They have a pointed snout and, like the spadefoots, are not commonly encountered. The most familiar toads, however, are the "true toads," the short-legged, warty "hop toads" often seen around homes and gardens. These toads are found throughout most of the United States and in Canada from central Alberta eastward through the southernmost provinces.

Characteristics

The hallmark of the true toad is its warts. The warts are actually glands that secrete an oily substance that keeps the toad's skin moist, helps prevent dehydration, and allows it to tolerate moderately dry conditions. Two larger glands, sometimes erroneously called poison glands, are located on the back above the toad's shoulders. These glands secrete a substance that, although not poisonous, irritates the eyes and mouth of predators and thus serves a protective function. Toads vary in size from less than ¼ inch (0.6 cm) to 3 inches (7.5 cm) or more when fully grown. They range in color from brown to reddish-brown to green, with their lower parts a lighter color, often a sandy brown. Darker spots might be present over the back, but the size and number of these vary. Since toads are short legged and heavy bodied, they get around by making short hops or by walking rather than using the long leaps characteristic of frogs. In all, the warts, short legs, humanlike hands, and plump body give toads an intriguing appearance and make them easily recognizable.

Habitat and Habits

The toad's habitat includes meadows, woodlands, river bottoms, lawns, gardens, and other similar places that provide adequate moisture and food. Being basically nocturnal, toads are most active at night and usually hide during the day by burying themselves in the soil. Most toads hibernate during the winter months, but they may be active year-round in the south.

Soon after emerging from hibernation, male toads travel to breeding pools—which may include ponds, swamps, marshes, river backwater areas, drainage ditches, or temporary ponds caused by rain—and begin their mating calls. Females, responding to the calls, make their way to the pools, where mating and egg laying occur. The adults then leave the pools to spend the remainder of the year in their usual haunts. Within a few days, the eggs hatch into tadpoles, which feed for several weeks on decaying vegetation and other bottom debris before transforming into tiny housefly-sized toads. At the end of this transformation, the young toads leave the pools and take up a terrestrial existence.

Obtaining Food

Toads are voracious eaters and feed primarily on insects, insect larvae, earthworms, and other small invertebrates. The food must be alive, since it is movement that attracts a toad's attention and stimulates it to feed. Once a toad spots its food, it normally sits quietly and awaits the approach of the prey. Then the toad flips out its moist tongue, to which the prey sticks, then immediately retracts it and swallows the food whole. To make swallowing easier, the toad draws its eyeballs deep into their sockets, which are open to the roof of the mouth. This helps move the food to the throat region and gives the toad a blinking appearance as it swallows. Although toads are nocturnal, it is interesting to note that they sometimes sit under an outdoor light where they can easily catch insects that hit the light and fall to the ground.

Toads in the Classroom

Given the proper environment, toads adjust well to captivity, are easy to care for, and are interesting to observe. It is especially interesting to watch them capture and consume their prey—or miss and try again. And since toads exhibit numerous adaptations to their special way of life, they can be the focus of many observations and discussions of the relationship between animals and their environment. However, as mentioned earlier, toads require large amounts of food, so anyone planning to keep one should be prepared to provide for this need.

How to Obtain

In the spring, when they are calling from their breeding pools, toads can easily be located at night with a flashlight and picked up by hand. At other times, they might be found around gardens, flower beds, or near a porch or street light when they come out in the evening or at night to catch their prey. Toads can also be purchased from some biological supply companies (see Resources, page 226) and occasionally from pet shops.

Caring for Toads

Housing   Toads are very easy to care for in captivity because their needs are relatively simple and easy to meet. A standard terrarium is a satisfactory enclosure for toads, but they tend to uproot the vegetation when they dig. A modified terrarium is, therefore, a more satisfactory arrangement, as digging will not disturb the plant roots. Toads are more tolerant of dry conditions than other amphibians, but they can lose moisture through the skin and suffer from dehydration if the environment is too dry.

Toad in a modified terrarium

Since toads do not drink water but rather absorb moisture through the skin, the terrarium soil should be kept moist, and a shallow, stable dish of fresh water should be provided in which the toad can soak. The toad will adjust to the moisture level of its environment by varying the amount of time it spends in the water. While probably not necessary to prevent escape, a glass or wooden cover will help maintain a suitable humidity level.

Diet   Toads will eat a variety of insects, and their appetite is seemingly insatiable. One can be kept quite busy catching enough insects to satisfy a single toad for an extended period. For this reason alone, toads do not make good long-term captives unless one is prepared to capture, raise, or purchase a large number of insects for food. On a short-term basis, though, catching insects or purchasing them locally is not too much of a task. Insects that crawl or walk are easier for the toad to catch than those that leap or fly. Crickets and mealworms, for example, are fairly easy to obtain and make excellent food, but grasshoppers, although good food and easy to obtain, would be more difficult for the toad to catch. Most toads will also accept earthworms and some other invertebrates, such as ants and pill bugs.

In nature, a toad might go for several days without harm if it cannot find its insect prey. Thus it is possible to leave a captive toad over weekends or short vacations of three or four days without feeding it if all its other environmental needs are met. But to prepare a toad for these periods of fasting, it should be fed daily whenever possible.

Some Tips on Feeding   Feed a toad by simply dropping one insect at a time into the cage near the toad. If several are offered at once, the toad will become distracted by the various movements of the insects. This phenomenon can easily be observed through experimentation. Also, as mentioned earlier, toads feed only on living organisms; this is not because they can tell the difference at a glance, but because the organism's movement stimulates the toad's feeding response. This can be demonstrated by offering the toad a dead insect—it will not be eaten. But if you loosely tie another dead insect on a thread and dangle it in front of the toad, the toad will probably eat it. One can capitalize on this phenomenon when natural food is not available by feeding the toad insect-sized bits of meat in the same way.

A Note on Handling

Generally, it is best not to handle a toad any more than is needed. But when it is necessary to do so, a toad can be gently picked up and held in one or both cupped hands. Alternatively, the toad can be encouraged to hop into a small container for holding or observation. In either case, care should be taken to prevent it from falling.

When the Project Is Over

See page 10 in Chapter 1 for suggestions on what to do with animals that are no longer wanted or needed in the classroom.

Observations, Activities, and Questions

- Observe and describe a toad. Can you find the ears and nostrils? Are all the skin glands (warts) the same size? Are they all the same color? Where do most of the skin glands appear? How many toes does a toad have on the front feet? How many are on the hind feet?

- Describe how a toad catches and swallows its prey. How does it use its tongue, feet, and eyes when it eats?

- Does a toad seem to have a favorite resting or hiding spot in its cage?

- Observe and describe how a toad burrows into the soil.

- Place a toad on the floor and describe how it moves.

- Determine the breathing rate of a toad by counting the number of times its throat moves in one minute.

Tiger Salamanders

Background

Tiger salamanders are widespread in the United States, from Canada south to the Rio Grande and the Gulf of Mexico and—with the exception of the Appalachian highlands and the Northeastern states—from the Rocky Mountains east to the Atlantic Coast.

Characteristics

Tiger salamanders are the largest of the terrestrial salamanders, and the heavy-bodied adults reach a length of 8 to 9 inches (20–23 cm). About half of the tiger salamander's total length consists of the laterally flattened tail. The head is broad and flattened, with widely set eyes and a wide mouth containing numerous but harmless small teeth. The tiger salamander's ground color is usually dark brown to black, and the body is generously covered with yellow to olive-brown spots of irregular size and shape.

Habits and Life Cycle

During the summer months, the adult tiger salamanders live in woodlands, forests, prairies, and open fields. Here they spend most of their time burrowing in the leaf litter and soil, where they find their natural diet of insects, insect larvae, and earthworms. Because of their burrowing nature and secretive habits, they are rarely seen during the summer and are sometimes referred to as "mole salamanders." They are much more visible and commonly seen in the early spring, when the adults migrate to marshes, ponds, and prairie potholes to mate and lay eggs before returning to their terrestrial way of life. The eggs are typically deposited in clusters of six to twenty or more and are usually attached to a weed or twig. The eggs hatch within a few days into aquatic juveniles, which, except for the presence of gills, look very much like tiny adults. Unlike the tadpoles of frogs and toads, the salamander larvae are predators of water fleas (daphnia), mosquito larvae, and other small aquatic organisms. The larvae grow to a length of 3 to 4 inches (8–10 cm) before losing their gills and transforming into the adult stage. This growth and transformation usually requires one summer, but it may require two seasons in the northern part of the salamander's range where the summers are shorter.

Although the major migration to and from the breeding pools occurs in early spring, tiger salamanders are sometimes stimulated to move about by periods of rainfall and may be seen at such times. During their periods of activity, and especially in the spring, tiger salamanders are sometimes found in basements, garages, or window wells. This is especially true when new houses have been constructed on a migration route of the salamander or near a breeding pool. In this case, a salamander may wander inside the house while attempting to find its way around the obstacle. If this should happen, the salamander can simply be removed and released a few feet (a meter or so) from the house—or taken to school. During the winter months, salamanders hibernate in underground tunnels or in the burrows of other animals.

Tiger Salamanders in the Classroom

Tiger salamanders adjust quickly to classroom conditions, are hardy, and are easy to maintain in captivity. They show the typical salamander attributes, and being larger than most other salamanders, they are easy to observe and study.

How to Obtain

Tiger salamanders can be obtained in a variety of ways. During times of migration or rainy periods, they can simply be picked up wherever they are encountered. They can also be captured with a net when they are in their breeding pools. The eggs can also be collected when they are available in the breeding pools. Of course, after the eggs hatch, the juveniles can be captured with a fine mesh net. Since tiger salamanders are occasionally used for fishing, they are sometimes available in bait shops. Tiger salamander eggs, juveniles, and adults are also available from some biological supply companies (see Resources, page 226).

Caring for Tiger Salamanders

Housing and Diet Any stage of the life cycle of tiger salamanders—eggs, larvae, or adults—can be kept in the classroom. A 5- or 10-gallon aquarium will be a satisfactory container for any stage, but the eggs and the larvae can also be maintained and observed easily in a 1-gallon jar. Salamander larvae, whether hatched from eggs in the classroom or collected directly from a pool, should be fed daily with daphnia or other similar aquatic organisms collected with an aquarium dip net. Since collecting live food every day or two can be time consuming and inconvenient, salamander larvae are troublesome to keep on a sustained basis, but they are exceptionally interesting to observe on a short-term basis. If one has the tenacity to provide sufficient food for them, the larvae will grow quickly and, in the warm indoor temperatures, will soon transform into adults.

Tiger salamander in a modified terrarium

Adult salamanders tend to burrow into the soil and uproot plants if kept in a terrarium and are thus difficult to observe. For this reason, a modified terrarium with a small amount of soil is better. But, in either case, the soil should be kept moist, and a dish of fresh water should be available at all times. Adult salamanders can also be kept in a 5- or 10-gallon aquarium with 1 to 2 inches (2.5–5 cm) of water. They do not need basking sites or other special appointments. Their food, consisting of mealworms, earthworms, or insects (such as crickets and darkling beetles), can be placed directly in the water, where it will be found and consumed. The salamanders will also learn to accept food held in forceps, and once they have learned this, they can also be fed strips of lean raw meat and fish. Any uneaten food should be removed so it will not decay and foul the water. Tiger salamanders, like other amphibians, can absorb toxic substances (even their own wastes) through their skin. It is therefore important to change the water regularly so these wastes cannot accumulate.

Adult salamanders do not have to eat on a daily basis. They also adjust easily to moderate temperature fluctuations, so they can be left over weekends and short vacations without special attention—as long as their moisture needs are met.

A Note on Handling

An adult tiger salamander can be picked up by wrapping the fingers around its body and using the thumb to prevent it from wiggling free. Salamander larvae should be handled with an aquarium net just as one would handle fish.

Salamander eggs should be kept under water but can be moved by maneuvering them into a small container.

When the Project Is Over

See page 10 in Chapter 1 for suggestions on what to do with animals that are no longer wanted or needed in the classroom.

Observations, Activities, and Questions

- Observe and describe a tiger salamander. How do tiger salamanders differ from other amphibians such as toads? How many toes do tiger salamanders have on the front and hind feet? Do tiger salamanders have webbing between the toes?

- Touch a tiger salamander and describe how it feels.

- Describe how a tiger salamander obtains and swallows its food.

- Place a tiger salamander on the floor and describe how it moves. Does it walk or leap?

- Determine the breathing rate of a tiger salamander by counting the number of times its throat moves in one minute.

Hatching Amphibian Eggs and Raising Tadpoles

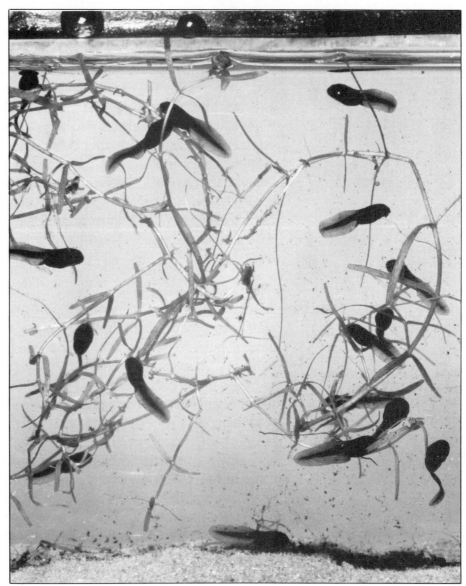

Most amphibians produce their eggs sometime in the spring, but the exact time depends on the locality, the weather conditions, and the kind of amphibian. An individual amphibian egg is small, about the size of an "o" on this page, but each egg is surrounded by a protein coat that swells when it comes in contact with the water. This gives the egg mass a gelatin-like appearance and usually makes it much larger than the amphibian that produced it. The number of eggs and the size of the egg mass depend on the species. The egg masses are usually attached to aquatic vegetation or submerged objects in shallow water along the shores of ponds and lakes.

Collecting Eggs

Amphibian eggs can normally be found a few days after the adults begin their mating calls. (Amphibian eggs can also be purchased from some biological supply companies — see Resources, page 226.) The egg masses are difficult to pick up. The easiest way to collect them is to trim off the attached vegetation and float the egg masses into a submerged bucket or plastic bag. Some additional water should also be collected for future maintenance of the eggs. As soon as possible after being collected, the eggs should be separated into smaller clusters of five to ten eggs and placed in individual containers. The developing embryos are especially susceptible to low amounts of oxygen and, if they are not separated, those in the center of the mass will die and eventually contaminate and kill the remaining eggs. Shallow dishes with just enough pond water to cover the eggs are all that is needed for hatching them.

Caring for Tadpoles

At room temperature, most amphibian eggs will hatch in five to seven days after being produced. Just before hatching, the embryos absorb the last remaining nutrient from the egg, so no food is needed for the next three or four days. At first, newly hatched tadpoles tend to be inactive and cling to the sides of the container (or, in nature, to any submerged object). Then they become more active and begin to feed. The natural food of frog and toad tadpoles is vegetation and decaying matter. In captivity, they can be fed pieces of lettuce, small bits of boiled egg yolk, or goldfish food. They will also graze on aquatic plants if they are available. (Salamander tadpoles, called *larvae,* are predators and must be fed as described on page 132.) It is important that the tadpoles not be overfed because the uneaten food will decay, foul the water, and reduce the oxygen level. If the water becomes cloudy, it should be changed immediately. Otherwise, it is advisable to pour off about one third of the water each day and then refill the container to its original level with pond water or aged tap water (see page 104). After one or two weeks the tadpoles can be transferred to more permanent quarters, such as an aquarium, and cared for much as one would goldfish, feeding them what they will consume and changing or adding water as needed. (Surplus or unwanted tadpoles should be released in the pool where the eggs were collected.)

Depending on the species, tadpoles grow and develop for two to three months before transforming into frogs or toads. During most of this time, the body is spherical with a tail that is two to three times longer than the body diameter. Tadpoles have a sucker-like mouth with rasping teeth and breathe through gills. The change from aquatic herbivores to terrestrial insectivores is a phenomenal event that involves both internal and external changes. The first noticeable change is the appearance of the hind legs. This occurs sometime before the actual transformation. Then forelegs appear and the tadpoles switch from gill breathing to lung breathing. At this time the tadpoles (sometimes called "pollywogs" when they have four legs and a tail) must be able to crawl out of the water to prevent drowning. They will not eat for the next few days because their internal organs are continuing to transform. At this time the tails are resorbed and gradually disappear. Following transformation, the juveniles can be housed and maintained in the same manner as the adults.

Salamander larvae look like miniature adult salamanders except that they have visible gills. Transformation in salamanders involves simply resorbing the gills and moving to land.

Careful observation of an amphibian's life cycle and daily record keeping by students will enhance their understanding and appreciation of this developmental process.

When the Project Is Over

See page 10 in Chapter 1 for suggestions on what to do with animals that are no longer wanted or needed in the classroom.

Chapter 8

Reptiles

The word *reptile* elicits many thoughts and attitudes. Some are positive but, unfortunately, many are negative. Some people fear and hate reptiles; others describe them as slimy or creepy. All in all, reptiles are probably the most misunderstood of all the world's creatures. The opportunity to correct some of these misconceptions may be reason enough to study them, but reptiles are also fascinating in their own right. As an ancient group, they represent the branch of the evolutionary tree from which both the birds and the mammals developed. Knowledge of living reptiles—their biology and adaptations—can be the basis for sound ecological understandings, and nothing can help to alleviate fears or remove misconceptions associated with reptiles more than close-up study of them.

Reptiles of the Past

Living reptiles are only a remnant of a greater past. Their origin is clouded by time and by the fact that early reptile fossils are similar to those of the amphibians from which they evolved. But evolve they did, to dominate not only the land as dinosaurs, but also the sea as ichthyosaurs (fishlike lizards) and the air as pterodactyls (winged lizards). They evolved to fill many major ecological roles. Some of the giant dinosaurs, over 90 feet (27 m) long and weighing more than 50 tons (45 t), were herbivores that fed on the often lush vegetation of primeval swamps. Others were carnivores, preying on the herbivores and smaller carnivores. The giant reptiles reached their prominence during the Age of Reptiles, which started some 200 million years ago and lasted until about 65 million years ago. Many theories have been offered to explain the decline of the great dinosaurs, but all of them are conjecture; no one really knows the reason.

Today's Reptiles

Today there are only a few kinds of reptiles compared with the past: snakes; lizards; turtles; crocodiles; and the rare, primitive tuatara, found only on islands off the coast of New Zealand. But even within these few kinds, there is considerable variation. Turtles, for example, range in size from the 3-inch (7.5-cm) Eastern mud turtle to the giant leatherback sea turtle, which can exceed 7 feet (210 cm) and 1,600 pounds (720 kg). Some snakes are fully grown at 10 inches (25 cm), but the anaconda can exceed 30 feet (9 m). Some crocodiles exceed 20 feet (6 m) and occasionally a specimen will reach 30 feet (9 m). Most lizard species are fairly small, but some are larger, with the Komodo dragon exceeding 12 feet (3.6 m). The tuatara, a 2-foot (60-cm)-long species with three eyes, is a direct descendant of the dinosaurs and is the most unusual living reptile.

Characteristics

Diverse as they are, living reptiles have certain characteristics in common—features that define their group. First, they are *ectothermic* (coldblooded), which is often thought to be a disadvantage. However, reptiles have developed a variety of behavioral ways to contend with their cold-bloodedness and can maintain a fairly stable internal temperature even in widely fluctuating environmental temperatures. For example, they bask in the sun to warm up or retire to the shade to cool off. Many desert reptiles are active at night to avoid the daytime heat, or they are active in the evening to avoid either day or night temperature extremes. But, then, being ectothermic is not necessarily a disadvantage. Reptiles do not waste a lot of food energy to produce body heat. This means that they do not need to eat regularly, and, in many cases, they can go for extended periods without eating at all—a distinct advantage in times of food shortages. And the only thing that is required to survive the winter months is a secure place to hibernate.

The Land Egg   One of the great contributions of the early reptiles, and one of the things that make them reptiles, was the development of the "land egg." Most amphibians are limited by their need to return to the water to complete the reproductive cycle. The land egg, which has special membranes that reduce water loss, freed the reptiles from the need to return to the water to reproduce and allowed them to "conquer the land." The land egg became the basis of the evolution of both the birds and the mammals. A hen's egg today, for example, is not very different from a dinosaur egg 200 million years ago, and, except for the shell, the internal egg of modern mammals is structurally very similar to the reptile egg from which it evolved.

An interesting thing about reptile eggs is that, like the animals that lay them, they, too, are ectothermic. This means that the eggs do not have to be kept at a specific temperature in order to hatch. Birds incubate their eggs for two, three, or four weeks, but most reptiles simply lay their eggs and leave them. If the temperature happens to be warm, the eggs hatch quickly; if it is cooler, the incubation period is longer. Some snakes, such as the garter snake, do not lay the eggs but rather retain them within the body until they hatch, and then they give birth to live young—a system reminiscent of mammals. In either case, the young are always self-sufficient, thus relieving the adults of any parental care.

Reptile Skin   Another interesting feature of reptiles is their skin, which is generally thick, tough, dry, and covered or partially covered with scales. While often considered to be slimy, reptile skin does not even have the glands that could moisten it. In fact, reptile skin is impervious to water, which prevents water loss and helps make it possible for reptiles to live under exceptionally dry conditions. The amount of skin covered by scales depends on the kind of reptile. Snakes, lizards, and crocodiles are almost completely covered by scales. Turtles' skin is less scaly, with much of the flexible skin around the legs being relatively free of scales. Most reptiles shed their skin as they grow. Many people are familiar with the shed skin of a snake. This is not the complete skin but rather just the outermost layer, or *cuticle*. An examination of a shed skin will reveal the details of the underlying skin, including the scales. It is this layer, the cuticle, that is water resistant and therefore dry.

Some other reptile features worthy of note are that reptiles breathe through lungs, most have a three-chambered heart (crocodiles have a four-chambered heart), and their eggs are internally fertilized.

Is It Poisonous?   The first question that is often asked about a snake— Is it poisonous?—may reflect the basis for much of the negative feeling toward reptiles. Actually, not many North American reptile species are poisonous. Those that are include four kinds of snakes (rattlesnakes, water moccasins or cottonmouths, coral snakes, and copperheads) and two lizards (Gila monsters and beaded lizards). Bites from the poisonous lizards are rare, but serious. Venomous snakebites do occur but are usually not fatal if appropriate action is taken. Even though venomous snakebites are infrequent and the survival rate is high, poisonous snakebites can result in severe tissue and muscle damage. At the very best, venomous snakebites can cause extremely painful, slow-healing wounds.

Desert collared lizard

Selecting Reptiles for the Classroom

The first point to be made about selecting reptiles for the classroom is that *poisonous reptiles should not be kept at school.* The risk is simply too high. Venomous reptiles are truly fascinating, and the temptation to keep one can sometimes be great. But even with the best of care and intentions, accidents can occur. Even a locked cage must be opened for feeding and cleaning, and this presents a potential danger to the keeper. Also, snakes are notorious escape artists.

Many snakes, turtles, and lizards are easy to keep in captivity, but others are less practical to keep in the classroom because of their size, temperament, feeding requirements, or other special needs. Some kinds of snakes—for example, bull snakes, pine snakes, and rat snakes—tend to be fairly docile, but most water snakes and racers have rather nasty dispositions and are more difficult to handle. The food of some snakes is readily available and easy to provide, while other snakes have more specialized diets. Most garter snakes, for example, can be maintained on a diet of earthworms and minnows, both of which can be collected locally or purchased from a fish-bait shop. Queen snakes, on the other hand, which closely resemble garter snakes and are often mistaken for them, feed almost exclusively on soft-shelled (newly molted) crayfish; and Eastern hognose snakes feed almost exclusively on toads. These specialized diets make both of these snakes difficult to maintain in captivity. Also, snakes that feed on small mammals may not be appropriate for the elementary classroom because of the practical aspects of providing live food, as well as the potential traumatizing effect this type of feeding could have on students.

All else considered, smaller reptiles that are easy to handle and maintain are more appropriate as classroom animals. Virtually all the important reptilian characteristics and behavioral patterns can be easily observed in the smaller reptile species. Also, smaller reptiles tend to be less threatening to those who feel uncertain about them.

In any case, it is important to identify a prospective classroom reptile accurately in order to eliminate any venomous specimens and to ensure that the captive receives proper care.

Garter Snakes

Background

There are several kinds of garter snakes. Collectively, they are the most widespread and probably the best-known of all North American snakes. They are found throughout most of the United States, and some range into the southern part of Canada. The preferred habitats of garter snakes are as varied as their large geographic range implies. They can be found in wet lowlands, woodlands, meadows, relatively dry grasslands, mountain valleys, rocky outcrops, and practically any combination of these habitats except high, barren mountains.

Characteristics

Although the color and markings can vary considerably, a "typical" garter snake has either greenish or reddish-brown to black ground color and three longitudinal stripes—one on the midline of the back and one on each side of the body. The belly coloration is normally similar to that of the stripes. In most species, there are also two small, but distinct, light spots on the top of the head. These snakes are relatively small, with most adults being from 18 to 26 inches (46–66 cm) in length (although some garter snakes can be larger).

The diet of garter snakes is relatively constant among the various species, with earthworms, amphibians, and fish being the mainstay. (Most garter snakes will not eat insects, as is often thought.) Like all other snakes, garter snakes swallow their food whole—without chewing it—and they do not "unlock their jaw" in order to swallow large prey. They are able to swallow surprisingly large prey because of the flexibility of the skull and jaw and the special way the jaw is hinged.

Garter snakes can tolerate a wide range of temperatures and are consequently active from early spring until late autumn. They do prefer warm temperatures, though, so they tend to be most active, and are most often seen, during the warmer parts of the day. They can control their body temperature somewhat by basking in the sun, so they are inclined, especially on cool autumn days, to crawl out on a warm rock or a black road surface to warm themselves in the sun (the latter choice often resulting in their demise).

Garter snakes pass the winter months in hibernation, sometimes singly and sometimes in large aggregations called *snake balls*, which might include several kinds of snakes all wrapped together. Their hibernation sites include cracks and crevices in rocks or foundations, rock piles, ant mounds, open wells, and abandoned buildings. The snakes usually converge and enter these sites unnoticed in the last weeks of fall. Most of them emerge in the spring on the same day, and this is a spectacular event. Sometimes hundreds of snakes can be seen at these times as they move slowly about, soaking up their first rays of sun. During the summer they might move several miles (kilometers) from the hibernation site, but they usually return to the same site at season's end.

Reproduction

Garter snakes mate soon after emerging from hibernation, when there are lots of snakes in one place and it is easy to find a mate. Unlike most other reptiles, garter snakes give birth to live young by retaining the eggs (which do not have hard shells) in the body until they hatch. Then the young are released from the female's body in what appears to be live birth. A female typically produces 20 to 30 young at a time but may produce many more.

Defending Themselves

Garter snakes are preyed upon by a variety of other animals, including mammals, large birds, and even other snakes. Their major means of defense is to escape through the vegetation, which they can do with surprising speed. If caught, however, they whip the body violently and release a foul-smelling, and presumably foul-tasting, musk from a gland near the anus. When they are first caught by a human, they react in the same way, often leaving the musk on the hands of the captor. However, if handled regularly and gently, garter snakes become quite docile.

Garter Snakes in the Classroom

Easily maintained as captives, garter snakes make good classroom animals. Furthermore, their presence in the room can help alleviate many of the uncertainties, misunderstandings, and superstitions that children often have about snakes.

How to Obtain

Although garter snakes are widespread and often abundant, it can sometimes be difficult to find one in nature because they are secretive and well camouflaged. However, when a garter snake is encountered, it can simply be picked up and transported to school. Otherwise, garter snakes can be purchased from some biological supply companies (see Resources, page 226) and, occasionally, from a local pet store.

Caring for Garter Snakes

Housing   Garter snakes can be kept in a variety of cages; but whatever type is selected, it should have good ventilation, smooth interior walls, adequate visibility, a secure cover, and plenty of space. Either a standard aquarium or a similar-sized wooden cage with a glass front (see Figure 2-9 on page 19) is ideal if fitted with a secure, ventilated cover. A wood-framed screen cover is fine for the cover, but never use wire screen, even for ventilation holes, at floor level, as the snake will rub its nose against the rough screen and injure itself. Garter snakes can be kept in a planted or modified terrarium, but they tend to crawl over the plants and destroy them. A sterile terrarium is probably best for garter snakes, but it should be equipped with a forked stick for climbing and a rough rock or two that the snake can

Garter snake in a sterile terrarium

rub against when shedding its skin. Paper towels spread flat on the cage floor make the most suitable substrate. They are absorbent, which will keep the cage dry (a necessity for garter snakes), and can be easily changed as needed. Sand or soil is less desirable since either material makes cleaning the cage difficult. Wood shavings should not be used because chips can be ingested with food and cause internal injuries to the snake.

Fresh water should be provided daily in an open, shallow dish that is not easily tipped. This will provide drinking water and will also allow the snake to soak itself occasionally.

Diet   The natural diet of most garter snakes consists of amphibians, fish, and earthworms, and any of these will be accepted in captivity. It is important, however, to exercise good judgement about the size of the food offered. All snakes swallow their food whole, and, although snakes can swallow surprisingly large objects, a small garter snake cannot eat a large frog. But the size of the food is not the only consideration. Garter snakes do not kill their prey before swallowing it, and the struggle between a snake and its prey can be gruesome to observe, especially for elementary school children. For this reason, it is better not to use amphibians for snake food.

Most garter snakes can be maintained on a diet of earthworms, which can easily be collected or obtained from a bait shop or pet store. Earthworms can also be raised as a classroom project (see page 35). Simply place the earthworms, one at a time, in the cage in front of the snake. Most garter snakes will also learn to catch small live minnows placed in their water dish. Many specimens will also accept strips of raw fish. A sustained diet of fish, however, is inadequate for garter snakes and would need to be supplemented with earthworms.

It is difficult to recommend the proper amount to feed a garter snake because of the possible variation in size of the snake and the kind of food being offered. It is best, therefore, to determine amounts through experimentation; but keep in mind that snakes rarely overeat. Finally, snakes do not need to eat daily, and a good meal once or twice a week is adequate. These eating habits, combined with their wide temperature tolerance, make garter snakes especially easy to keep over weekends (but you must be sure they never run out of water).

About Shedding All snakes shed their skin as they grow. During periods of rapid growth, this may occur several times in a season. Just prior to shedding, a snake's eyes become cloudy, it typically refuses to eat, and it may become more lethargic than usual. Shedding begins around the mouth, and the snake simply crawls out of its skin, leaving it wrongside out. In nature, the snake crawls through the vegetation to facilitate the shedding process. In captivity, the snake will rub against a stick, rock, or other available object to accomplish the same result.

A Note on Handling

The first or second time a garter snake is handled, it will attempt to escape and might try to bite. Therefore, it should be held securely with one hand just behind the head and the other hand supporting the rest of the body. After being handled a few times, most garter snakes become quite docile and can be handled more casually. However, all but very small snakes should be held with both hands to provide as much support as possible and to prevent them from thrashing about. In all cases, a snake should be held firmly and care should be taken to prevent it from falling.

When the Project Is Over

See page 10 in Chapter 1 for suggestions on what to do with animals that are no longer wanted or needed in the classroom.

Observations, Activities, and Questions

- Observe and describe a garter snake. How many stripes does it have? Where do the stripes begin and end? Does it have any spots or stripes on the head? How do the scales on the bottom differ from those on the sides and top? Can you find the nostrils? Does the garter snake have ears? Does it ever close its eyes?

- Describe how a garter snake moves.

- Describe how a garter snake catches and swallows its prey.

- Why does a garter snake stick out its tongue? How many times does it stick out its tongue in one minute?

- If a garter snake sheds its skin, examine it carefully. Note the individual scales, including the eye scales.

Green Anoles
(American Chameleons)

Background

Green anoles, sometimes called American chameleons, are found in the southern states, from Texas eastward along the Gulf of Mexico and north through part of North Carolina. However, these small, attractive lizards are so readily available through pet stores and biological supply companies and appear so often as pets in elementary school classrooms that they deserve consideration as a representative lizard. This is especially true since, in spite of the best intentions of the keeper, many anoles die because inappropriate information about them leads to improper care. For example, at one time it was popular to recommend sugar water as adequate food for these insectivorous animals. Of course, anoles fed in this way would soon die of malnutrition.

Characteristics

As the erroneously applied common name "chameleon" suggests, these small, slender lizards, 5 to 8 inches (13–20 cm) long, have the ability to change their color. (True chameleons, the masters of color change, are native to Africa.) Green anoles are usually solid green on top, but the color can change to mottled green-brown or solid brown, depending on the animal's mood and the environmental temperature. The lizard's chin and underparts are white (this does not change), and adult males have a pink throat, which can be expanded into a "throat fan" to signal other anoles.

In nature, anoles live among the twigs and leaves of shrubs and small trees, where they pursue their insect prey and obtain water by licking raindrops or dew from the foliage. Anoles appear to adjust readily to the presence of humans and are as likely to be found among landscape plantings around homes, even in cities, as in more undisturbed areas. Since anoles obtain both their food and water from foliage, they are inclined to spend most of their time in the vegetation, but they are also seen on the ground.

Male anoles are territorial, which means they defend a certain area of their habitat from intrusion by other males of the species. However, the males rarely fight. Rather, an anole signals "ownership" of a certain area by extending its pink throat into a fan-shaped structure, then raising and lowering its head. The rate of this movement indicates the intensity of the anole's feelings, and this behavior usually results in the retreat of the intruder to another area without further interaction between the two males.

Reproduction

The throat fan is also used as a signal between male and female anoles as part of the mating ritual. After mating, the female deposits two to four eggs in leaf litter, under pieces of bark, or in cracks and crevices. The eggs hatch in a few weeks, and the young take up an existence among the vegetation similar to that of the adults.

Green Anoles in the the Classroom

Apart from being easy to care for, green anoles are especially interesting because of their ability to change color. They demonstrate a variety of biological and ecological concepts, such as camouflage and predation, as they hide among the vegetation and capture their insect prey. Since they show the typical lizard characteristics and are interesting and innocuous, they are nice representative reptiles for classroom studies.

How to Obtain

In regions where they occur in nature, green anoles can be found and captured among or around the vegetation where they normally live. Otherwise, they are commonly available through pet stores and from some biological supply companies (see Resources, page 226).

Caring for Green Anoles

Housing   Green anoles can be kept in a sterile terrarium with a branching twig on which they can climb. However, a planted terrarium or a modified terrarium (see pages 15 and 16) will provide a much more natural environment for them, since they normally climb and hide among vegetation. A 10-

Green anole in a planted
terrarium

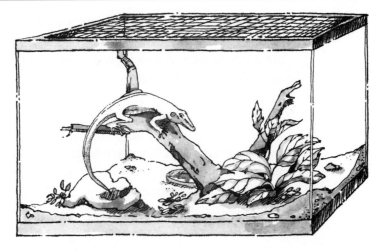

gallon aquarium (or larger) makes an ideal-sized enclosure for an anole or two, but it should be provided with a tight-fitting screen cover to prevent escapes and allow for ventilation. For a planted terrarium, 1 to 2 inches (2.5–5 cm) of soil in the bottom of the aquarium will provide a medium in which any houseplant that is appropriate in size—except for cacti—can be planted to give the anoles a perch and hiding area. A sturdy, branching twig should also be supplied for perching, basking, and displaying. Finally, while not necessary, a piece of bark, a rock or two, and some moss will add to the attractiveness of the anoles' quarters.

Once established, the anoles and their terrarium will be easy to maintain. In general, an environment that supports the plants will be satisfactory for the anoles. Sprinkling enough water over the plants every day or two to sustain them will provide enough water for the anoles, since they drink directly from the water droplets on the leaves. Of course, the terrarium should be kept where the light is adequate for plant growth.

Diet   Anoles are insect eaters and will accept only live, moving insects of an appropriate size. Mealworms are an excellent food and are easy to obtain, but because the exoskeleton is indigestible, a sustained diet of them may cause digestive problems. However, the white mealworm larvae, which have just shed their skins, are ideal and can be used whenever they are available. Mealworm larvae can also be raised in the classroom (see page 66). Anoles will also accept flies, small crickets, and other soft-bodied insects, including small caterpillars and insect larvae that climb on twigs and leaves. The food can simply be placed in the terrarium, where the anoles will find it, but most anoles will also learn to accept wiggling insects from forceps.

One should not have to clean the anoles' terrarium often. Their small, dry fecal pellets will not be objectionable and will decompose in the soil. Of course, any dead insects should be removed, as these will not be consumed and are slow to decay.

Anoles do not hibernate; they simply become lethargic during cool periods. They are reasonably tolerant of changes in temperature and can, therefore, be kept in classrooms with fluctuating weekend temperatures. Finally, although daily feeding is recommended, anoles can go without food for a day or two. A few extra live insects left in the terrarium will provide weekend forage for them.

A Note on Handling

When first captured or handled, anoles will attempt to escape, so they must be grasped quickly. They are fragile, however, so care must be exercised not to harm them. To capture an anole, quickly place one hand over it and curl the fingers around its body. Take care not to catch it by the tail if it attempts to dart away, and never pick one up by the tail.

When the Project Is Over

See page 10 in Chapter 1 for suggestions on what to do with animals that are no longer wanted or needed in the classroom.

Observations, Activities, and Questions

- Observe and describe an anole. What color is it? Is it the same color all over? How many toes does it have on the front and hind feet? Describe the toes.

- Describe how an anole moves its eyes. Do the eyes move together or independently?

- Describe how anoles catch and eat their prey.

- Place an anole in the dark for about an hour. What color does it become? Does it change color when it is returned to the light? How long does this take?

Painted Turtles

Background

Painted turtles are the most widespread and probably best-known of all North American turtles. They are found throughout most of the United States (except in the southern tier of states where they are rare or absent) and are the most abundant of all turtles in the northern states and southern regions of the Canadian provinces.

Characteristics

The *carapace* (upper shell) of painted turtles is generally smooth and, except for an intricate lacelike pattern of red, yellow, or black along the margin, is drab olive to gray in color. The head, neck, legs, feet, and tail are olive-green to black with bold yellow or reddish-yellow stripes. The *plastron* (lower shell), also yellow to reddish-yellow, is plain in eastern specimens but has a dark central blotch in the western forms. Painted turtles range in size from about 1 inch (2.5 cm) at hatching to 6 to 7 inches (15–18 cm) as adults.

Although painted turtles occasionally wander about on land, they are primarily aquatic and seem to prefer quiet, shallow water with abundant submerged vegetation. Marshes, swamps, ponds, roadside ditches, river backwaters, and even the shallow margins of larger lakes can all support high concentrations of painted turtles if their simple requirements are met.

Painted turtle food consists largely of the aquatic vegetation in which they hide and the abundant insects and snails that live in this vegetation.

These turtles are strongly inclined to bask in the sun and will climb on any available object to do so. In the absence of these sites, the turtles will bask by floating at the surface of the water. While basking, they are especially wary and will slide into the water and hide among the vegetation if disturbed. Otherwise, they are curious and will sometimes swim close to a boat or dock to observe any activity there.

Painted turtles are active during the warm summer months, but long before the water freezes, they will bury themselves in the muddy bottom of their home pool, where they hibernate until late spring.

Reproduction

Mating occurs soon after the turtles emerge from hibernation, and the females then journey onto land, where they bury their clutch of six to ten eggs in the soil. The eggs normally hatch after six to eight weeks, and the young make their way to the water where they, like the adults, feed on aquatic vegetation, insects, and snails.

Painted Turtles in the Classroom

In many ways, turtles are unusual animals. Keeping and studying a painted turtle in the classroom will provide students with the opportunity to make many interesting observations about them including their structure, adaptations, and behavior. Properly kept, these turtles are both safe and easy to maintain.

How to Obtain

When painted turtles are moving about on land, they can simply be picked up by hand. Since they can swim fast and often hide among the aquatic vegetation, they can be most easily caught with a long-handled net (such as a fish landing net) when in the water. Because of concerns about disease transmission, turtles are not as commonly available from pet stores as in the past. However, painted turtles or similar species are available from some biological supply companies (see Resources, page 226).

Caring for Painted Turtles

Housing   Since painted turtles are primarily aquatic, a classroom turtle should be housed in a container in which it can submerge itself completely in water. But it should also have the opportunity to leave the water at will. A 10-gallon aquarium with 3 to 5 inches (8–13 cm) of water and a rock (or a brick or an inverted flowerpot or water bowl) that extends above the waterline is a simple arrangement that meets the turtle's needs and is easy to maintain. Since turtles are messy eaters, the ease with which the enclosure can be cleaned is an important consideration. An aquarium-terrarium arrangement (see page 17) will be more aesthetically appealing and will meet the needs of smaller painted turtles. However, larger turtles will climb over and destroy most terrarium plants, so they are probably best kept in the aquarium environment described above.

Painted turtles do well in a normal classroom environment (even if the temperature is reduced over weekends). However, they seem to prefer

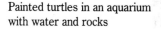
Painted turtles in an aquarium with water and rocks

warmer temperatures and will thrive in a warm part of the classroom. If cool temperatures are thought to be a problem, a lamp positioned above the basking rock will allow the turtle to warm itself.

Diet In captivity, painted turtles will consume any of their natural foods, including certain aquatic vegetation, insects, and snails. These items are sometimes difficult to provide, so mealworms, earthworms, and small strips of fish or lean meat are appropriate substitutes. The food can simply be placed in the water, but any food not consumed within an hour or two should be removed to prevent its decaying and fouling the environment. After two or three feedings, one can easily estimate the proper amount of food to provide. These turtles will also quickly learn to take food from forceps. This is a good feeding technique because, once the turtles have learned it, they will demonstrate when they've had enough to eat by losing interest in the food being offered. Normally, at least some food should be offered each day, but these turtles can easily go two or three days without feeding, so weekend care is easy to provide with a good feeding on Friday.

Long-Term Captivity Turtles are an excellent example of animals that are easily kept for two or three weeks but present greater problems if kept for extended periods. Though the foods mentioned above will sustain turtles adequately for a short time, they might not satisfy the turtles' long-term nutritional needs—for example, turtles need calcium, which is lacking in mealworms, and vitamin D, which they normally produce by basking. Therefore, if painted turtles are kept for more than one month, their diet should be fortified with vitamin and mineral supplements. Furthermore, some specimens may become lethargic during the winter months, when they normally hibernate. At this time, they might refuse to eat, and, if so, their health will decline and they will be more of a burden than a valuable classroom resource.

A Note on Disease

Turtles can carry salmonella bacteria, the cause of salmonellosis in humans. This is normally not a problem if hands are washed immediately after handling a turtle or cleaning its enclosure. Since the bacteria are eliminated with the feces, removal of the droppings and frequent changing of the water is recommended, not only for the well-being of the turtle but also to reduce the possibility of spreading the disease. Although the danger of disease can be reduced, it is probably most prudent to have students observe but not handle captive turtles. Also check local health regulations before you decide to keep a turtle in school.

When the Project Is Over

See page 10 in Chapter 1 for suggestions on what to do with animals that are no longer wanted or needed in the classroom.

Observations, Activities, and Questions

- Observe and describe a painted turtle. What color is the carapace (the upper shell)? What color is the plastron (the lower shell)? Are there stripes on the head, neck, and legs? What color are they? How many toes does the turtle have? Are the toes webbed? Are there claws on the toes?
- Describe how a painted turtle obtains and eats its food.
- Describe how a painted turtle walks.
- Describe how a painted turtle swims.

Box Turtles

Background

There are several kinds of box turtles in the United States. They differ only slightly in appearance, but since they occupy different habitats, they have slightly different environmental needs and food preferences. Box turtles are found in appropriate habitats throughout the eastern and central United States, from southern Maine westward to South Dakota, then southwestward to Arizona.

Characteristics

The box turtle is renowned, and appropriately named, for its ability to pull in its head, feet, and tail and close its shell for protection. This feat can be accomplished because the turtle's high, dome-shaped *carapace* (upper shell) provides room for its appendages and because the *plastron* (lower shell) is hinged, allowing the two halves to be pulled upward and held tightly closed. This shell makes the box turtle the best protected of all North American turtles.

In turtles, there is an apparent relationship between the amount of protection provided by the shell and the relative aggressiveness of the species. The snapping turtle, for example, has a reduced plastron and consequently less protection from its shell, but this is more than made up for by its aggressiveness. Conversely, the complete protection afforded the box turtle by its shell is reflected in its retiring and docile nature.

The shape of the carapace and the degree of protection it provides is reminiscent of the giant tortoise and characterizes the box turtle as being primarily terrestrial. The short, stumpy legs and small feet, and the lack of webbing between the toes are also terrestrial adaptations. The toes are equipped with strong claws for digging in the soil.

The box turtle's shell is usually black or brown and is typically marked with yellow to orange spots or streaks. However, the markings are highly variable. Some box turtles have few or no markings, while in others the lighter colors are so profuse that the shell appears to be yellow or orange with irregular dark markings. Markings on the head, neck, and legs are equally variable.

The eyes of young box turtles are normally brown, but in mature males the eyes are often red. Females rarely have red eyes. This fact helps determine the gender of a box turtle but is not totally reliable because of its variability. Another sexual difference, which is also variable, is that the rear lobe of the plastron is slightly concave in males to allow closer contact during mating. These two characteristics taken together usually make it possible to identify males and females.

Habitat

River bottoms, moist forests, and woodlands are typical habitats for Eastern box turtles. Western species are more tolerant of dry conditions and are more likely to be found in open areas. Box turtles are active throughout the warm months but are most conspicuous during the spring and fall as they wander about in search of food. In the summer, they avoid the midday heat by limiting their activity to the morning and evening hours. During extended dry periods, they bury themselves in moist soil or mud or soak in shallow water, sometimes for days at a time. In the cool days of fall, they bury themselves in soft soil or enter the burrows of other animals, where they hibernate until spring.

Reproduction

Box turtles typically mate in the spring soon after they emerge from hibernation. Then, in June or July, the female lays from three to eight leathery-shelled eggs in a nest she excavates in the soil. The eggs normally hatch in two to three months, just in time for the juveniles to enter hibernation. The young turtles usually go into hibernation without feeding, so little or no growth occurs until the following year. Juvenile box turtles are very secretive, so little is known of their early growth and activity. However, they appear to grow slowly, reaching sexual maturity and a length of 3 inches (7.5 cm) in about 5 years; 4 inches (10 cm) in 12 to 15 years; and 5 inches (12.5 cm) in about 20 years. At this point, growth becomes very slow, although box turtles commonly reach 60 years of age, and some may live for over 100 years.

Obtaining Food

Box turtles eat a wide variety of plant and animal materials, but they are opportunistic feeders and generally consume whatever is available to them at a particular time. Their food consists of mushrooms, insects, snails, earthworms, dead animals, and various fruits and berries.

Defense Reaction

When a box turtle is first encountered in the wild, its first line of defense is to withdraw into and close its shell. Any attempt to encourage a turtle to open up by prodding will be futile. The only way to get one to come out is to leave it undisturbed for several minutes. It will then follow a predictable pattern of behavior and come out in its own time—turtle time, which is slow. First, the shell opens slightly, and the turtle peeks out. If convinced of its safety, the turtle opens its shell more and pokes out its head. After carefully looking around, it opens even more and slowly extends its feet. Finally, if there is no disturbance, the turtle will wander off and go about its normal activity.

The entire process might take a turtle 15 to 30 minutes, but if there is any disturbance, the entire procedure will start again. However, after a short time in captivity, this strong protective response diminishes, and most specimens will withdraw only when strongly provoked.

Box Turtles in the Classroom

Box turtles adjust nicely to captivity. Their needs are simple and easy to meet. They are more active and alert than most other turtles and even show signs of intelligence. As such, they make interesting captives and are more commonly kept as pets than most other turtles.

How to Obtain

Box turtles can be found and simply picked up wherever they are encountered in nature. (Before attempting to obtain a turtle from its natural habitat, check with your state's wildlife agency to determine if it is a protected species. For the agency's address, see page 227.) However, since they are secretive and often burrow into the soil or become inactive during dry periods, they are sometimes difficult to find. As a result, the best way to find box turtles is to actively search their natural habitats at appropriate times. A team of searchers will enhance the chance of success. Box turtles are occasionally seen crossing a road or highway where they can be easily picked up. Box turtles are also sometimes available in pet stores but are usually not available from biological supply companies.

Caring for Box Turtles

Housing   A medium to large aquarium is an ideal enclosure because of the visibility it gives, but a wooden box or a child's plastic wading pool is also suitable for box turtles. If the container is about three times the height of

Box turtle in an aquarium with soil and a water container

the turtle, no cover is needed. Otherwise, a screen cover should be provided. The enclosure should contain 2 to 3 inches (5–7.5 cm) of moist soil and a water container that is larger than the turtle's body. The water container will serve as a source of drinking water and also as a place for the turtle to soak itself. If the water container is more than 2 inches (5 cm) deep, put some rocks or gravel in the bottom to assist the turtle in climbing out. Then fill the outside enclosure with soil to about the top of the water container. The soil will provide a comfortable substrate and a medium in which the turtle can bury itself, which is part of its regular routine.

Diet   Captive box turtles should be offered food resembling their natural diet. Most box turtles will readily accept earthworms, crickets, and mealworms, all of which can easily be collected, raised in the classroom (see pages 35, 51, and 66), or purchased locally. As a substitute for these live animal foods, small (insect-sized) strips of lean raw meat or hamburger are acceptable. Some specimens will also learn to accept canned dog and cat food. They should also be offered a variety of vegetables, including lettuce, and fruits, such as apple, muskmelon, and banana. The food preference and the amounts consumed will vary, so one should not be alarmed if some of these items are not accepted or if the turtle does not seem to eat much. Also, a box turtle might not choose to eat on a regular basis, but infrequent meals will meet its needs as long as a sufficient quantity of food is kept available. The key to success in keeping a box turtle is to offer it a variety of foods and let it select its own diet. If the turtle has not eaten after two or three weeks, however, it should be released at the point of capture.

Since box turtles are opportunistic eaters and naturally undergo periods of fasting, depending on the availability of food, they can be left over weekends and short vacations without being fed. However, water should always be available.

Long-Term Captivity   If a box turtle is being kept over the winter, it might burrow into the soil and remain inactive for extended periods of time—perhaps for a month or two. There are two reasons for this. First, the turtle's biological clock is probably telling it that it is time to hibernate. Second, the shorter days and cool nights (and weekends, if the heat is reduced) tend to reinforce the biological clock mechanism. Since a classroom is not cool enough for hibernation for the entire winter, the turtle should not be allowed to remain inactive for too long. If this phenomenon is noticed, the cage temperature should be increased to 70°–80° F (21°–27° C) by suspending a light bulb near one end of the cage and adjusting its height to produce the desired temperature. The constant temperature and light will reduce the turtle's desire to hibernate and stimulate it to eat.

Since keeping a box turtle over the winter presents these special problems, it is probably in the best interest of both keeper and captive to release the turtle before cold weather starts, either at the point of capture or in some other suitable habitat.

A Note on Disease

Box turtles, like other turtles, carry salmonella bacteria, the cause of salmonellosis in humans. It is therefore recommended that hands be carefully washed immediately after handling or feeding a turtle or cleaning its cage. Since the bacteria are eliminated with the feces, removal of the droppings and frequent changing of the water is recommended. This will reduce the possibility of spreading the disease and also contribute to the well-being of the turtle. Although the danger of disease can be reduced, it is probably prudent to have students observe but not handle turtles. Also check local health regulations before you decide to keep a turtle in the classroom.

When the Project Is Over

See page 10 in Chapter 1 for suggestions on what to do with animals that are no longer wanted or needed in the classroom.

Observations, Activities, and Questions

- Observe and describe a box turtle. Note the color and location of any markings. How many toes does the turtle have on the front and hind feet? Does it have claws on all of the toes? Can you find the nostrils and ears?

- Encourage a box turtle to withdraw into its shell by gently touching it on the head and feet with a folded strip of paper. Then examine it carefully. Can you see the head, feet, and tail? Ask the teacher to turn the turtle over; then look for the hinge on the plastron (lower shell).

- Observe and describe how a box turtle eats and swallows its food.

- Place an object such as a pencil near one of the box turtle's eyes. Do the eyes blink together or independently?

Hatching Snake and Turtle Eggs

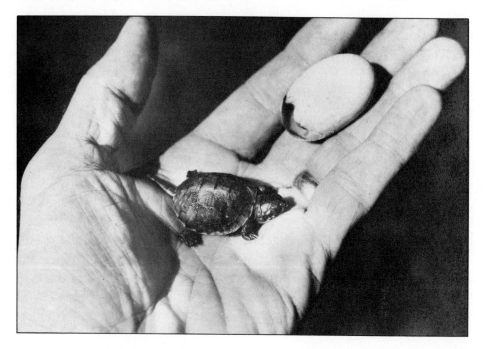

Hatching Methods

Turtle eggs in a plastic bag

When a snake or turtle being kept in the classroom lays eggs, the occasion will generate considerable excitement. This is not an uncommon event, particularly if the animal is a turtle that was picked up in the spring as it was wandering about prior to nesting. (Note: Before attempting to obtain a turtle in its natural habitat, check with your state's wildlife agency to determine if it is a protected species. For the agency's address, see page 227.) It is interesting to observe reptile eggs and compare their size, shape, and texture with the more familiar eggs of birds. Even more interesting is the possibility of hatching the eggs.

Hatching most snake or turtle eggs is a simple matter and may be accomplished in several ways. Two methods are described here. The first involves hatching the eggs in a plastic bag, which has the advantage of allowing observation of the eggs without disturbing them. To begin, moisten two or three paper towels and a handful of sphagnum moss or some vermiculite. Squeeze out the material as thoroughly as possible and then form it into a cup-shaped nest in the bottom of a thin plastic bag. Next, arrange the eggs in a single layer in the nest. Then close and secure the bag with a fastener placed as high as possible on the bag so that an air space is present above the eggs. The bag can be opened as needed to add water or, if it is too wet, to allow some moisture to escape.

Another method of hatching that works especially well for turtles involves burying the eggs. (This method, however, does not allow for observation of the eggs.) Bury the eggs 2 to 3 inches (5–7.5 cm) deep in sandy soil (a mixture of peat and sand works well) or vermiculite in a pail or large can that has holes punched in the bottom for drainage. Water the soil as needed to keep it moist but not wet. The holes will allow excess water to drain out and help moderate the moisture content of the soil. When the young turtles hatch, they will dig to the surface and wander about, so the top of the soil should be 3 to 4 inches (7.5–10 cm) below the rim of the container to prevent escapes.

Important Considerations

Four factors—temperature, moisture, mold prevention, and care of the hatchlings—should be considered when hatching reptile eggs.

Temperature   A precise temperature is not critical for hatching most reptile eggs. Temperatures from 70° to 90° F (22°–32° C) will do; room temperature is therefore satisfactory. The important consideration, as far as temperature is concerned, is that the eggs should not be chilled or overheated either before or during the incubation process, and the temperature should not be allowed to change too suddenly.

Moisture   It is important to keep the eggs moist to prevent dehydration, but too much water should be avoided. A good rule of thumb is to keep the eggs only slightly moist, but if they start to dehydrate, as evidenced by a slight indentation of the flexible shell, a small amount of water should be sprinkled on the paper towels.

Mold Prevention   Any time an organic material is exposed to high humidity and moderate temperatures it is susceptible to molds. Reptile eggs are no exception. The best way to help prevent mold growth is to keep the eggs as dry as possible without allowing them to dehydrate. However, if mold does develop, it should be carefully brushed or scraped off the eggs (using a toothbrush or a dull knife), and the medium should be replaced. This might have to be done three or four times during incubation.

Care of the Hatchlings   The final consideration, that of caring for the young, is also a simple matter. During the final stages of development, reptiles absorb a large amount of yolk, which sustains them for a long time. Therefore, the young will not require food for a week or two. (In nature, they sometimes enter hibernation without eating.) At this time, they should either be released in a suitable habitat or provided with the proper food. Most young turtles consume the same food as the adults. The diet of young snakes is more varied and depends on the species involved; some will consume earthworms, others will accept insects or mealworms. Of course, the proper environment should be provided for the young, and water should be available at all times.

One should not expect all the eggs to hatch since some might not be fertile. Also, reptiles eggs require a long time to hatch—in some cases as long as three months. Even after the eggs begin to open, several days may pass before the young emerge.

Record keeping by students will enhance the value of hatching reptile eggs in the classroom. Students can record the beginning and ending dates to determine the duration of the incubation period. They should also record any care provided during this time as well as their observations of the hatching process.

Chapter 9   *Birds*

Because they are vocal, colorful, active, and relatively abundant, birds are more visible and better known than most other animals. When asked to identify a characteristic of birds, most people comment on their ability to fly. Bird flight has fascinated humans and captured their imaginations since early times. Not all birds fly, however, and there are many other animals, including insects and bats, that can fly. A characteristic that is unique to birds is the presence of feathers; all birds have them, and there are no other animals that do.

Birds got their start millions of years ago during the height of the Age of Reptiles. They apparently evolved from a line of small dinosaurs that walked on two legs. The oldest bird fossil discovered was so similar to some of these dinosaurs that it was first thought to be one. It was not until the discovery of an identical fossil with feather imprints that the difference was recognized. Today, modern birds continue to retain certain reptilian characteristics, including scales on the legs, certain skeletal features, and their method of reproduction—egg laying.

The ability to fly makes many demands on birds, and being especially adept at the skill, they had to make several adaptations to make flight possible. First and most obvious was the need for wings, but using the forelegs as wings meant that birds had to be able to stand, walk, perch, and, in some cases, catch their food with only two legs. Efficient flight also required a lightweight and compact body. Birds accomplished this in a number of ways: their bones are hollow; they have a lightweight yet strong beak instead of heavy teeth; and their heavier internal organs are clustered under their wings. Flight also required strength and high energy. To fill this need, birds developed strong chest muscles and the most efficient respiratory system of all animals. In order to function effectively, both of these systems require heat. Birds are able to maintain a high body temperature because

they are *endothermic* (warmblooded) and have one of nature's best insulators—feathers. Finally, flying, hunting from the air, and landing required good eyesight, another quality birds developed to a high degree.

Reproduction

Birds inherited their system of reproduction almost intact from the reptiles. A bird egg is very similar to a reptile egg. Although the shells may differ, the inside of a bird egg (the part that develops into a new individual) is very similar to that of a reptile. A major difference, however, is that bird eggs, unlike reptile eggs, must be maintained at a consistently warm temperature in order to hatch. This means two things: first, the adult birds must *incubate* (sit on and hatch) the eggs; second, they must construct a place to do so—a nest. Rearing the young generally follows one of two patterns that are related to the size of the egg and the length of the incubation period. An egg must contain all of the nutrients for the developing embryo. A relatively large egg, which contains a lot of food, allows the developing bird to remain in the egg longer. As a result, the young bird will be more fully developed when it hatches. These young, called *precocial*, are usually able to feed themselves and require minimal parental care. Chickens, ducks, and pheasants have this type of egg development. On the other hand, eggs that contain a small amount of food must hatch sooner, when the young are at an earlier stage of development. These less mature young, called *altricial*, require considerably more parental care. Altricial development is characteristic of (but not confined to) robins, sparrows, doves, and most other smaller birds.

Habitats and Habits

Today, as measured by their diversity and adaptability, birds are very successful animals. They are found in almost every habitat, from the tropics to arctic regions, and exploit almost every conceivable food source. On land, they may be found in a range of environments, from rain forests to deserts. Some birds, such as loons, are almost totally aquatic. A few, like the wandering albatross, soar endlessly—twenty-four hours a day—over the ocean, scooping their food from the water and coming to land only to raise their young. Some birds, such as hawks and owls, are predators; others, such as parrots, are primarily vegetarian. Birds vary in size and weight from tiny hummingbirds no larger than a moth to the flightless ostriches that can exceed 300 pounds (135 kg). This seemingly endless variety makes birds an especially interesting group of animals to study.

Selecting Birds for the Classroom

Fascinating as they are, several factors limit the kinds of birds that are appropriate to keep in the classroom. First, almost all native birds, as well as some introduced ones, are protected by federal and state laws. It is illegal to possess them, their nests, or their eggs without special permits. This is just as well, since wild birds are inappropriate for the classroom. These legal restrictions limits the selection to a few domesticated birds and those that are available through the pet trade.

Most of the common domesticated birds, such as ducks, geese, and chickens, are simply too large and too messy to make satisfactory classroom animals. The smaller bantam chickens, however, have some potential for classroom use, especially if a hen is used to incubate a clutch of eggs.

A variety of birds are available through the pet trade, but most of these are inappropriate as classroom animals under normal circumstances. Most of the smaller cage birds that are often kept in homes, such as canaries, finches, and parakeets, are easily alarmed and do not adjust well to the activity of a classroom. An even greater problem is that many of these birds do not adjust to the temperature fluctuations that sometimes occur in classrooms overnight and on weekends during the winter months. These birds are also susceptible to diseases, especially when under the stress that might occur in a classroom. The larger parrots and parrotlike birds can also be a problem in the classroom for the reasons noted for the smaller birds and also because they are sometimes noisy and distracting. Special knowledge is also required to care for them properly. All of this is not to imply that these birds cannot or should not be kept at school, but unless the teacher has the time, the facilities, and the special knowledge and skills to care for them, they are not good choices as classroom animals.

Although most birds are either unsatisfactory or impractical for the classroom, one group has characteristics that make them suitable for classroom study. These are the doves, especially ring doves, that are available from pet stores. These birds seem to adjust well to classroom conditions. They are also relatively easy to care for and will go through their entire reproductive cycle in the confines of a cage.

Doves

Background

Various kinds of doves are found in tropical and subtropical regions around the world. Some of them are widely kept for food or as pets. Only a few kinds are found in North America and most of these occur in the southern-most areas. One, however, the mourning dove, is widespread and can be found throughout most of the United States and southern Canada. Another, the ring dove, is one of the more commonly available pet doves, and one that is especially suitable for the classroom.

Characteristics

Ring doves have a light gray back and are cream-colored underneath. A dark ring, which partially (and sometimes completely) surrounds the neck, gives them a distinctive appearance, as well as their name. These birds have been kept in captivity for so long, and have been released and become established in so many places, that their original range is unknown. Since their introduction to the United States, they have become established in several southern cities.

Doves resemble small pigeons but are somewhat more slender and have a long, pointed tail. Although they usually nest in trees, they are rarely found in deep forests. They prefer more open areas and are often found in small woodlots and fence rows along fields. They spend a lot of time on the ground, where they search for food, and are also frequently seen perching on utility lines along roadsides. They seem to thrive in the presence of humans and, being especially adaptable, are common in suburban areas, where lawns serve as feeding areas and trees and shrubs provide nest sites. Evergreen trees seem to be favorite nest sites. Doves' nests are constructed of a few twigs and are notoriously flimsy. Sometimes they are so thinly constructed that the eggs are visible from below. As a result of this poor nest construction, many nests are lost during storms, and sometimes the eggs simply roll out or fall through the nest. But doves are persistent nesters, and if one nest is lost or if one brood has been raised, they will renest and sometimes complete several reproductive cycles in one season.

Another interesting and unique feature of doves (and their close relatives, the pigeons) is their method of feeding the young. They feed the young "crop milk," sometimes called "pigeon milk," a substance resembling cottage cheese that is secreted by the *crop* (a space in the throat) of the adults. During the incubation period, in which both the male and female participate, their crops begin to develop into glands that start producing the milk about the time of hatching. At first the young, called squabs, are fed pure crop milk, but as they mature, they are given some seeds and, later, seeds alone.

Obtaining Food

Adult doves feed almost exclusively on seeds although occasionally an insect may be eaten. Weed seeds are the mainstay of the diet, but doves are opportunistic and will eat many kinds of grains when they are available. In agricultural areas, they often glean fields following the harvest or consume spilled grain around storage areas.

Doves and pigeons have an ability that is unique in the bird world. Typically, when birds drink water they fill their beak with water and then raise their head so that the water will run down their throat. Doves and pigeons are the only birds that are able to suck water into their crop against the force of gravity.

Ring Doves in the Classroom

Although the widespread and familiar mourning doves are protected and cannot be kept in captivity, ring doves are in many respects ideal classroom animals. They are easy to care for, quiet, clean, and, with normal care, do not cause offensive odors. Being *endothermic* (warmblooded), they thrive at normal room temperatures and easily adjust to lower evening and weekend temperatures. If given a sufficient supply of food and water, they do not require special attention over weekends and short vacations.

How to Obtain

Ring doves can be purchased from pet stores. A hobbyist (who might be located through a pet store) might also be a source of these birds.

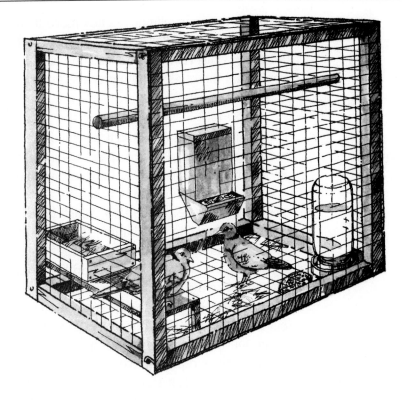

Ring doves in a multipurpose wire cage

Caring for Ring Doves

Housing   A wood or wire multipurpose cage (see Figures 2-7 and 2-8 on page 19) is satisfactory for a pair of ring doves but should be as large as possible in all dimensions. Since these birds are primarily ground dwelling, the cage should have a floor space of at least 2 by 4 feet (60 x 120 cm) and sides at least 3 feet (90 cm) high. A perch (a wooden dowel or a branch) should be securely attached to the sides of the cage. If a breeding pair is being kept, a four- or five-inch (10–12.5-cm) diameter bowl or a similar-sized shallow wooden box should be provided for a nest site. This will be utilized if placed on the floor of the cage but can also be attached securely to a shelf in the cage. Straw, fine twigs, pine needles, or dried grass should also be made available for nest building.

Diet   Dove ration in the form of pellets or mixed grain is usually available from pet or feed stores. Alternatively, the wild bird seed mixture that is normally available at grocery stores is an excellent food, especially if supplemented with split peas. The food should be provided in a heavy dish, a gravity-flow food hopper, or a chick feeder (see Figures 2–12, 2–13, and 2–15 on page 21). Doves need a source of calcium for egg production as well as a source of grit to aid digestion. Both of these needs can be met by providing commercial bird grit (calcium-based) in a separate container. Grit is also available from pet or feed stores. Fresh water should also be provided in a water fountain or a heavy bowl (see Figure 2–18 on page 22 and Figure 2–12 on page 21).

A Note
on Handling

It is best not to handle doves any more than is needed. However, when it is necessary to handle them, they should be held firmly to prevent escapes. With the wings restrained, place one hand around the body and wings from above and the other hand under the breast.

Breeding
Ring Doves

There are four stages in the reproductive cycle of ring doves, and both the male and the female participate in each phase. The first stage involves courtship and nest site selection. In this phase, the male struts, bows, and coos as the female watches passively. After a day or two of this, the pair selects a nest site. Stage two, which lasts about one week, involves nest building and mating. Incubation, the third stage, begins with egg laying and ends with hatching. Normally, two eggs are laid—the first usually in the late afternoon and the second about 36 hours later. The female incubates the eggs most of the time, but the male normally takes over from about 10:00 a.m. until 4:00 p.m. each day. Incubation lasts about 14 days, but since one egg is laid before the other, the eggs will hatch about a day and a half apart. Stage four, rearing the young, normally lasts about three weeks.

The entire reproductive cycle takes about six weeks, but, sometimes, even before the last stage ends, the male begins to strut and coo, and another cycle will be underway. Thus it is possible for a single pair of ring doves to complete eight nesting cycles in a year. Typically, however, they do not do so. Even indoors, ring doves will sometimes have a longer resting period between cycles during the winter months.

When studying ring doves, it is sometimes useful to be able to distinguish between males and females. Since both sexes are identical in appearance, the only way they can be identified is through their behavior—the male struts and coos and only incubates the eggs during the midday hours. During one of these identifiable times, it is a good idea to mark one of the pair with a leg band or a piece of soft yarn. (Leg bands are usually available at pet stores.)

When the
Project Is Over

See page 10 in Chapter 1 for suggestions on what to do with animals that are no longer wanted or needed in the classroom.

Observations, Activities, and Questions

- Observe and describe a ring dove. Note the color of its beak, feet, and eyes, as well as any markings on the feathers.

- If a pair of doves is being kept, mark one of them for individual identification by loosely tying a piece of soft yarn around one of its legs. Then observe and record the interaction between the two doves. Do both of the doves coo? Does one seem to demonstrate dominant behavior? Which seems to spend more time sitting on the eggs? After hatching, do both of the adults care for the young? Observe the young doves daily and record any changes.

Hatching Bird Eggs and Caring for the Young

Environmental Conditions

Bird eggs require three environmental conditions in order to hatch: a specific and constant temperature, a high humidity, and a specific amount of time. When eggs are laid, the embryos are dormant. A temperature of 99° to 103° F (37°–39° C) is required in order to break the dormancy and initiate embryonic development. Then, since the embryos cannot produce their own heat, the eggs must be incubated (kept warm) at about body temperature (bird temperature) until they hatch. Eggs are typically about 60 percent water. This water is essential to the developing embryo. However, under dry conditions the water will gradually evaporate through the porous shell, resulting in problems at hatching time or, possibly, death of the embryo. Successful hatching therefore requires that the eggs be kept under humid conditions. The time required for hatching varies with each species. In general, smaller birds have a fairly short incubation period, and the time increases as the size of the bird increases. An adult bird provides for all of the needs of its eggs: warmth comes from its body, moisture comes from its skin, and, of course, the bird instinctively sits on the eggs until they are ready to hatch.

While not an environmental factor, another requirement for successful hatching is the rotation of the eggs on a reasonably regular basis. If the eggs are not rotated, the embryo and its associated membranes may adhere to each other and to the shell, resulting in difficulty at hatching time. This rotation is accomplished naturally by adult birds as they move over the eggs. In some species, the adults deliberately move the eggs with their beaks.

Hatching Eggs in the Classroom

Hatching eggs in the classroom without adult birds requires that attention be given to all of these factors—temperature, humidity, time, and rotation of the eggs. The most practical way to control the first two is with an artificial incubator; the time factor is a matter of patience; and rotation of the eggs should be done at least two times each day (including weekends, if practical).

Several styles of incubators are available from biological supply companies (see Resources, page 226) or from local sources. Many science books also give instructions on how to build an incubator. Whatever type is used, though, incubators with a thermostatically controlled heat source are much more reliable and easier to use than those without one.

Obtaining Eggs   Although any kind of bird egg can be hatched artificially, it is only practical to incubate those of the precocial type so that the young, upon hatching, can feed themselves. Altricial hatchlings require intensive parental care and would soon die if they were incubated in the classroom. Chicken eggs are a good choice for classroom incubation because they are more readily available than others. And because they are precocial, the chicks are relatively easy to care for. Quail and pheasant eggs are sometimes available, but the young are a little more difficult to care for and sometimes require a special permit. Domestic ducks and geese can also be hatched in an incubator, but they are especially messy to maintain.

Fertile chicken eggs can sometimes be obtained from a local farmer, hobbyist, or commercial hatchery. If not, they can be purchased from some biological supply companies. Once obtained, the eggs can be stored at room temperature or even in a refrigerator for a few days, but after ten days to two weeks the viability might decline.

Before Starting   There is no need to hatch more eggs than necessary to provide an interesting learning experience. Hatching too many eggs will increase the space and maintenance needs of the chicks. But, since some eggs might be infertile and not hatch, enough eggs should be incubated to achieve success. Ten or twelve eggs is a good compromise.

Before obtaining the eggs, one should give consideration to caring for the young birds in the classroom and to finding a suitable home for them when the project is finished.

Baby chickens are not difficult to maintain but will require an appropriate enclosure with a temperature control system and special food. When they get older, chickens become more troublesome in the classroom because they need considerably more space, eat a lot of food, and are sometimes noisy. Their cages also require regular cleaning. For these reasons, it is generally best not to keep baby chickens in the classroom more than one or two weeks.

If you obtain eggs from a local source, the young can sometimes be returned there. Also, a person who raises chickens might be willing to accept chicks. *Unless a good home can be found for the young birds where they will receive responsible care, the project should not be undertaken.*

Incubator Operation:

1. Before placing the eggs in the incubator, adjust the temperature to about 100° F (38° C). The acceptable range is 99° to 103° F (37°–39° C). Keep a thermometer in the incubator and check it regularly to make certain that the temperature has stabilized. Then lock or tape the control knob of the thermostat in place to prevent accidental movement.

2. Place a shallow pan of water in the incubator. The water will slowly evaporate and provide the needed humidity. Refill the container as needed so that it is not permitted to become dry.

3. Using a pencil or water-soluble pen, mark the side of each egg to make a reference point and place the eggs in the incubator, marked side up. Then, each time the eggs are turned, place the mark alternately down and then up. It is not actually necessary to rotate the eggs 180° each time, but this system helps ensure that each egg gets turned. After the eighteenth day, the eggs should not be rotated.

At Hatching   When the eggs begin to hatch on about the twentieth day, the chicks use a temporary sharp projection on their upper beak, called an *egg tooth*, to cut through the membranes and shell. This process is called *pipping*. The chicks continue to cut around the shell until it can be forced open. When they finally emerge, the chicks are wet and exhausted but quickly dry and can walk around within an hour. If a chick experiences difficulty in emerging from the egg, it is probably because of inadequate moisture or rotation of the egg. Unfortunately, it usually does little good to help the chick emerge at this point. Any eggs that have not hatched by the end of the twenty-first day probably will not do so. One should not expect all of the eggs to hatch. Hatching of 60 to 80 percent is good.

Housing and Care

After the chicks hatch, they must still be kept warm. They can be left in the incubator for a few hours but should then be transferred to an enclosure, or brooder, where the temperature is about 95° F (35° C). The temperature can then be reduced about 5° F (3° C) each week until room temperature is reached. Thereafter, a heat source is no longer needed.

Brooders can be purchased from a feed store or a biological supply company. A homemade brooder can be constructed by suspending a 60-watt light bulb with a reflector (aluminum foil) about six inches (15 cm) above the floor near one end of a large cage, cardboard box, or aquarium. This will establish a heat gradient, and the chicks will move closer or farther away from the bulb as needed to control their body temperature. If the chicks are too cool, they will huddle together and cheep a lot. In this case the bulb can be lowered or replaced with a 75-watt bulb. (Caution: The bulb should not be allowed to come in contact with any flammable surface.) Several layers of paper towels will provide an adequate substrate, and these can be removed one or two layers at a time to clean the cage.

Chicks in a cardboard box brooder

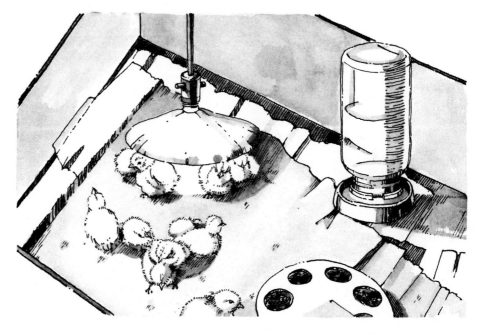

Just before the eggs hatch, the chicks absorb any remaining yolk. This meets their energy needs during the hatching process and for the next day or two. However, food and water should be provided from the outset so that the chicks will have an opportunity to find and gradually begin eating food before their reserves are depleted. Newly hatched chicks require food that has a high protein content. In nature or in the farmyard, they consume a large number of insects, insect larvae, and worms to satisfy this need. Artificially reared chicks should be fed chick starter ration, a special mixture that meets all their dietary needs. This is available from feed or farm supply stores or through biological supply companies.

Food is best provided in a chick feeder (see Figure 2–15 on page 21), but if one is not available, a heavy, shallow dish will do. Chicks consume a lot of water. This should be provided in a water fountain if possible (see Figure 2–18 on page 22). Fountains not only provide a reserve of clean water but are designed to prevent the chicks from falling in or fouling the water with droppings. If it is necessary to use an open dish for water, it should be partially filled with marbles or pebbles to prevent the chicks from drowning. The chicks can easily drink between the marbles, but the container will quickly become fouled and will have to be refilled often.

In order for students to gain the maximum benefit from this project, they should be encouraged to observe and record each step of the process. These records should include the beginning of incubation date and the hatching date as well as the daily readings of the incubator temperature. Students should also be encouraged to find pictures of chick embryo development. Studying these pictures and keeping their own data will enhance students' understanding of the developmental process.

Chapter 10 *Mammals*

Of all animals, mammals hold a special fascination for humans—perhaps because we are also mammals or perhaps because we are more familiar with them than with other animals. In fact, we are so accustomed to mammals that the word is synonymous with *animals* for many people. Small mammals are especially suitable to keep and study in the classroom. Being alert and active, they are more interesting to observe than more sedentary animals. Some mammals adjust well to classroom conditions and can be handled with ease. And, importantly, their needs are relatively easy to meet.

Mammals got their start millions of years ago, long before the extinction of the great dinosaurs. Then, as the dinosaurs declined, mammals proliferated and the Age of Mammals was under way. Many kinds of mammals have evolved through the milleniums, but most of them have become extinct. Today's mammals represent the top of the evolutionary line, the highest forms of life that have ever lived on earth.

Characteristics

Like other groups of animals, mammals are so diverse that it is somewhat difficult to describe them succinctly. Mammals range in size from a tiny shrew less than 2 inches (5 cm) long and weighing one fifth of an ounce (6 g) to the 150-ton (135-t) blue whale, which can reach lengths of over 100 feet (30 cm) and is probably the largest animal that has ever lived. Mammals have adapted to a variety of life styles. There are burrowing, running, jumping, climbing, flying, and swimming mammals. They can be *carnivorous* (meat-eating), *herbivorous* (plant-eating), or *omnivorous* (both meat- and plant-eating). They can be *diurnal* (active during the day), *nocturnal* (active at night), or *crepuscular* (active at dawn or dusk). They can be predators or prey.

Consistent with this great diversity, there are only a few characteristics that are distinctly mammalian. One of these is that mammals are the only animals that have hair. Their most outstanding characteristic is that they are the only animals that suckle their young—feed them milk from the mammary glands of the mother. This is their hallmark and the origin of the name of the group.

Reproduction

Another characteristic of interest is the mammals' method of reproduction. All mammals have internal fertilization, that is, the eggs are fertilized inside the mother. The typical pattern is that the eggs then become implanted in the uterus where the developing offspring are nourished through the placenta. The gestation period and the level of maturity of the newborns depend on the species involved. A notable exception to this pattern is found in mammals with pouches, such as kangaroos and opossums. After fertilization, the eggs develop in the uterus for a short time; then the young are born at an extremely immature stage. They crawl through the mother's hair, enter the pouch (the *marsupium*), and attach themselves to a mammary gland for several weeks of continued development. Another notable exception is found in the monotremes—the duckbilled platypus and the spiny anteater, both of Australia. Following fertilization in both of these unusual mammals, a shell forms around the embryo, just as in birds. The eggs are then laid and incubated in an underground burrow by the platypus and in the marsupial-like pouch by the anteater. After the young hatch, they feed on their mother's milk.

A characteristic that mammals share with birds is that they are *endothermic* (warmblooded). The ability to maintain a constant body temperature helps make mammals the active animals that they are, but there are exceptions even to this. Certain mammals, such as woodchucks and ground squirrels, are able to avoid the rigors of winter by hibernating—lowering their body temperature, thus reducing their energy consumption and the need to feed on a regular basis.

Selecting Mammals for the Classroom

Recommended Mammals   Several kinds of small mammals can be kept successfully in the classroom, but only a few are recommended. These are laboratory, or white, mice; laboratory rats; gerbils; hamsters; guinea pigs; and domestic rabbits. All of these are descendants of wild stock, but they have been domesticated for thousands of generations and can be safely handled. They can be cared for with relative ease, are generally free of disease, are adapted to living in the confines of a cage, and seem to adjust well to classroom conditions. Furthermore, because of their popularity, all of them are likely to be available from local sources— either a pet store or a private individual.

Other mammals can be kept at school, but before deciding to do so, one should review the criteria for animal selection outlined in Chapter 1 and then make the decision with caution. Not all mammals can adapt to classroom conditions, and many that will survive require an inordinate amount of attention and care or are unsuitable for other reasons.

Wild Mammals   Although the temptation to do so may be great, *wild mammals should not be kept in the classroom*. There is a difference between a domesticated animal and a "tame" wild animal. A domesticated animal is one that has been in human service for an extended time and has been bred to develop certain characteristics. These animals are used to human presence, are generally more docile and more easily handled, and, within reason, behave more predictably. A "tame" animal is usually one that has been taken from the wild or is a recent descendant of a wild animal. Although sometimes docile, it retains most, if not all, of its natural instincts. Instinctive behavior in wild animals is oriented toward survival. Responses such as aggression, defense, or escape can be triggered unintentionally by a touch, a loud noise, or a quick movement. These stimuli are likely to occur in a classroom. There are many accounts from owners of wild animals (raccoons, foxes, or squirrels) who said that their pets were really tame and then all a sudden went wild, forcing the owners to get rid of them. Or the pets were very tame when young, but as they got older, they become increasingly difficult to handle. Probably a better explanation is that the animals finally expressed their natural behavior, which had been suppressed in captivity. But either way, those experiences can be unpleasant, often involving bites, scratches, or hurt feelings and, perhaps, a trip to the doctor for shots. It would be extremely unfortunate if this situation occurred at school and involved an unsuspecting child.

Some wild mammals are also known carriers of diseases that can be transmitted to humans, including bubonic plague, carried mostly by rodents; tularemia (rabbit fever), transmitted by rabbits; leprosy, carried by armadillos; and rabies, which is usually associated with carnivores but which can also be transmitted by a variety of other animals. Then, too, some mammals are susceptible to certain human diseases, for example, respiratory diseases.

Another consideration is that most wild mammals are either nocturnal or crepuscular, so the captive animal's period of activity would not correspond to the school schedule. The animal would be active during the night (or at dawn or dusk) and would want to hide or sleep during the day, when students would be available to observe it.

Finally, most wild mammals, unlike most other animals, tend to be very active and occupy relatively large areas in nature. It is impossible to reproduce their environment in captivity, especially in the classroom. No one knows what stresses an animal undergoes when it is taken from its environment and confined in unnatural surroundings. It is probably a safe assumption, though, that confining an otherwise active mammal, especially a secretive, nocturnal one, in a small cage in a busy classroom is a potentially stressful situation.

Tame wild mammals may have a place at school—but only as visitors with an expert handler, not as classroom residents. All else being equal, domesticated mammals that are used to confinement, handling, and human activity are more suitable for the classroom situation and will provide meaningful learning experiences without the hazards and difficulty of dealing with wild mammals.

Other Considerations   One of the reasons for suggesting that mice, rats, gerbils, hamsters, guinea pigs, and rabbits are appropriate for the classroom is that they can all be handled by children. While being picked up is not a natural experience for animals, most of these animals will tolerate handling and become docile if handled regularly and properly. However, care should be taken not to handle the animals excessively, and they should always be handled gently. Anytime an animal is handled, there is a risk that it will bite. If it does, the bite should receive immediate treatment. Attention should also be given to reducing the anxiety of both the person bitten and the animal. And, if a bite (or for that matter, any other accident) occurs with an animal, it should be brought to the attention of the appropriate school authorities.

Mice, rats, hamsters, gerbils, and guinea pigs are all rodents and as such have two features that must be considered when keeping them in the classroom. Although rabbits are now classified separately, they were formerly grouped with the rodents because they share these two typically rodent features. One, rodents have large incisors that are used for gnawing. And, two, their incisors grow throughout their lives. While one of these features does not cause the other, the combined result is that the incisors grow at about the rate that they are worn away from growing. This balance of growth and wear keeps the teeth at about the right length when rodents have a normal diet and have the opportunity to gnaw. However, if a rabbit or rodent is prevented from gnawing, its incisors will become so long that it will not be able to eat. It is therefore essential that this phenomenon be considered when these animals are kept in the classroom. A proper diet, such as commercial rodent and rabbit chow that is compressed into firm pellets, will normally meet this need. However, it is a good idea to give these animals additional opportunities to gnaw by placing pieces of cardboard, wood, or twigs in their cages.

A strange phenomenon, and one that is disconcerting when it occurs, is that some adult animals, especially rodents, will occasionally consume their young. A number of reasons have been suggested for this, but no one really knows why it occurs. Some have suggested that a dietary deficiency is involved, but a disturbance, such as making a loud noise, picking up the parent or the young, or cleaning the cage, can trigger the action. Sometimes, part of an exceptionally large litter might be killed in what has been interpreted as an attempt to reduce the need for parental care or to improve the chances of survival of those not eaten. Whatever the cause, the likelihood of cannibalism can be reduced by keeping the animals in clean, spacious cages, providing plenty of nesting material, and providing a nutritious diet. In any case, anyone planning to breed animals in the classroom should be aware of the possibility of this unpleasant occurrence and be prepared to deal with it with students.

Like other animals, small mammals have varying degrees of vulnerability to disease. Hamsters and gerbils seem to be relatively free from disease problems. Mice, rats, guinea pigs, and rabbits, though, are more susceptible to respiratory diseases. These problems can usually be prevented by starting with healthy animals, keeping them in clean, dry, uncrowded, draft-free cages, and providing a proper diet. However, if an animal shows signs of problems, as indicated by loss of appetite, weight loss, breathing difficulty, or change in behavior, it should be isolated from other animals and removed from the classroom until its condition improves. (See *Animal Health,* page 7.)

A Special Note on Animal Reproduction

All the mammals described as being appropriate for the classroom (mice, rats, gerbils, hamsters, guinea pigs, and rabbits) have very high reproductive capacities, and all reproduce readily in captivity. However, classroom animals should not be allowed to reproduce more than is necessary to achieve the goals of the project. Unwanted animals cause problems because they need additional facilities and care and will eventually need appropriate homes. There are also ethical issues involved in allowing pets to produce unwanted offspring.

A person once suggested that the greatest problem in keeping mice in the classroom is disposing of the numerous young. The way to prevent this problem from arising is simple and applies to all animals—separate the males and females. One may keep animals without having them reproduce at all by selecting two of the same sex—preferably females, as they usually make more compatible cage mates than males. Alternatively, a single animal can be kept. If it is necessary to allow the animals to reproduce to achieve the goals of the class project, reproduction should be limited to only that which is necessary. This can be accomplished by separating the adults before the female gives birth to prevent them from mating again and by separating the juvenile males and females before the onset of maturity.

Before breeding any animals, be sure you have appropriate homes available for the offspring.

Mice

Background

Domesticated mice of the type kept as pets are descendants of the common house mouse. These small rodents are usually 3 to 3½ inches (7.5–9 cm) in body length and have a hairless tail that is typically somewhat shorter than the body. They weigh from 1 to 2 ounces (28–56 g), and their body shape varies from slender to plump, depending on their weight.

Because domesticated mice have been used so extensively in health-related research, they are sometimes known as "laboratory mice." And since most research labs use white specimens, these mice have also come to be known as "white mice." However, these mice can be a variety of colors or combinations of colors including black, brown, cinnamon, champagne, blue, and lilac. Mouse fanciers have also developed a variety of coat types, such as smooth, silky, and satin. But a mouse by any other name remains the same—call them all mice.

Even the name "house mouse" is something of a misnomer, since these mice certainly live in places other than houses. They are native to Asia, where they live in arid to semi-arid conditions and feed on a variety of seeds and insects. Some of the oldest human agricultural settlements have been discovered in Asia, and it is thought that the adaptable mice simply capitalized on the opportunity to share stored grain and other provisions of early humans and have been doing so ever since. (It is interesting to note that the word *mouse* comes from an old Sanskrit word meaning "thief.") As civilization expanded and goods were transported from place to place, the mice simply traveled along. Today, the house mouse is the most cosmopolitan of all mammals.

Even in today's less agrarian societies the house mouse is a ubiquitous human companion. In the absence of stored grain, mice simply adjust their diet and consume whatever food is available, including bread, cereal, candy, pet food, leftover foods, and garbage. Because of their adaptability, mice can live anywhere and, in fact, are found wherever humans live. With the possible exception of rats, mice probably represent the highest mammalian population of most cities.

Although mice are found wherever humans live, they can also live by themselves. Wherever they have been transported, they have wandered off and become established in the wild. This is especially true in arid or semi-arid regions that are similar to their native area. However, they also live in abandoned fields, rocky outcrops, and even in the tundra.

Reproduction

One of the reasons for the success of mice is their high reproductive potential. The life cycle is short. The gestation period is from 19 to 21 days, and the young reach sexual maturity in about 60 days. The litter size averages five or six, and a female can produce eight to ten litters in a year. Thus, the theoretical maximum number of mice produced in one year by a single pair of mice and their offspring is in the thousands.

When the young mice, called *pups*, are born, they are hairless and pink, their eyes are closed, and they are virtually helpless. They begin to grow hair after about one week, their eyes open at about two weeks, and they continue nursing until they are 25 to 30 days old. Individual mice might live for several years, but one to two years is more typical.

Destruction of Food

While mice seem to benefit from cohabitation with humans, the relationship is not a mutually desirable one. The amount of food a single mouse consumes is small and might not be missed. But mice usually do not live alone, and if sufficient food is available, the population will quickly increase. Loss of food to mice from a single home is not a major problem, but it is estimated that mice destroy thousands of tons of food and grain in storage facilities. Food that is not eaten is often fouled with droppings and urine when mice are present. Mice can also do considerable damage by gnawing and shredding clothing or bedding to make a nest. Mice have also been implicated in the transmission of a number of diseases, such as food poisoning, tularemia, ratbite fever, and plague. All in all, the total economic loss and human suffering caused by mice is phenomenal.

Contributions to Research

Mice have been used extensively in research programs related to human health and alleviation of pain and suffering. They have also been used in behavioral studies. Perhaps, in this way, laboratory mice have, at least in part, repaid the debt for the destruction caused by their wild relatives.

Mice in the Classroom

There are advantages and disadvantages to keeping mice in the classroom. They rank about equal with the other recommended small mammals in ease of care and handling. Being small, they require little space, which is a distinct advantage in a small or crowded classroom, and they require little food. While an occasional mouse is sometimes a little testy and inclined to bite, most become docile if handled on a regular basis. The biggest drawback to keeping mice is that their urine has a characteristic odor that can become especially unpleasant if the cage is not cleaned on a regular basis. Cleaning the cage twice each week, however, should keep the odor at an unobjectionable level. Of course, the amount of urine produced and the resulting odor is in proportion to the number of mice being kept. This might be a factor in deciding whether to keep a breeding pair and their offspring or just an individual or two.

How to Obtain

Mice are often available at local pet shops. Because of their popularity as pets, it might also be possible to obtain mice from a private individual — perhaps a student. In any case, be sure to select ones that appear alert and healthy. Mice are also available from some biological supply companies (see Resources, page 226).

Caring for Mice

Housing Mice can be kept in a variety of cages, including a commercial rodent cage, a 10-gallon aquarium with a secure screen cover, or one of the multipurpose cages shown in Figures 2-7, 2-8, and 2-9 on pages 00-00. A cage with a floor space of 10 by 14 inches (25 by 35 cm) is adequate for a pair of mice to raise a litter, but as the juveniles mature, more space will be needed. The floor of the cage should be covered with an inch (2.5 cm) or more of wood shavings or commercial pet litter. This will absorb moisture, help eliminate odor, and facilitate the cleaning of the cage. Two or three shredded paper towels should also be placed in the cage to provide nesting material. If sufficient nesting material is available, a nest box is not needed. However, if available, a small cardboard or wooden nest box, with a 1-inch (2.5-cm) square or round entrance hole, will be occupied by the mice. In this case, the nesting material should be placed in the box. An activity wheel, while not really necessary for their health, will be utilized by the mice and add a dimension of interest for students. In addition, a piece of wood placed in the cage will give the mice an opportunity to gnaw if they choose to do so.

Mice in a screen-covered aquarium

Diet   The best food for mice is commercial mouse or rodent chow, but dry dog food can also be used. Both of these foods can be supplemented with bird seed and occasional pieces of vegetable material such as carrots or lettuce. Whatever food is provided, at least some of it should be available at all times so that the mice can eat at will. It is best to suspend the food in a wire basket to prevent it from becoming fouled, but if it is necessary to feed the mice from a dish, a smaller amount of food should be offered. Because of the likelihood of contamination, any leftover food in the dish should be discarded and replaced each day.

Drinking water should also be available on a continual basis. Although their water consumption is minimal, mice usually drink at least some water each day, and the only practical way to provide it is with an inverted water bottle, which should be rinsed and refilled with fresh water frequently.

If provided with a sufficient quantity of food and water, mice can be left over weekends without further attention. For longer periods, some arrangements will need to be made for the animals' care.

A Note on Handling

The more mice are in the presence of humans, the tamer they will become and the more easily they can be handled. When they appear calm, they can be picked up by gently cupping both hands around them. Care should be taken not to squeeze them or confine them too tightly, though, as they might become uncomfortable and attempt to bite. At the same time, they should be confined sufficiently to prevent them from jumping or falling. Juvenile mice especially have no apparent knowledge or fear of heights and, if not controlled, will jump out of the hands and injure themselves.

Breeding Mice

Left to their own devices, a pair of mice will reproduce without special attention, but a few things should be considered. When selecting the mice, be sure to obtain one of each sex. Two mice, no matter how cute, will not reproduce if a mistake in identity has been made. It is difficult to determine the sex of mice, but an experienced person such as a pet dealer can help make an accurate selection. After placing the mice together, no special care, other than the normal day-to-day maintenance, is needed until just before the female gives birth. At that time and until the young are about one week old, it is best not to disturb the nest when cleaning the cage. Some books recommend removing the male before the young are born to prevent him from eating them. However, the male is no more likely to eat the young than the female. Most often, the male will be perfectly compatible and contribute to the care of the young by warming the nest. But the mice will sometimes mate again immediately after the young are born. To prevent this, remove the male before the young are born. Otherwise, it is only necessary to continue to provide food and water as usual, and the adults will care for their young.

The appearance and maturation of the young will be the same as that of the wild mice described earlier. When their eyes have opened, the young mice should be given the opportunity to investigate and nibble solid food. If they cannot reach the food bin, it should be lowered. Alternatively, an object (or more litter) can be placed in the cage for the young to climb on to reach the food. The water bottle should also be lowered to make it more accessible.

The juveniles will be weaned when they are 25 to 30 days old. They can be left with the adults for a while, but if the pair has mated again, the young should be transferred to another cage to prevent overcrowding. Remember that the mice become sexually mature at about 60 days of age. If the males and females are housed together, a population explosion might occur. Also, after maturity the males might fight each other, especially if housed together with females. One should therefore separate the sexes before they reach reproductive age. (See also *A Special Note on Animal Reproduction,* page 186.)

When the Project Is Over

See page 10 in Chapter 1 for suggestions on what to do with animals that are no longer wanted or needed in the classroom.

Observations, Activities, and Questions

- Observe and describe a mouse. Does it have whiskers? Does it have hair on its ears? Does it have hair on its tail? What color are its eyes?

- Record everything a mouse does in a certain period of time. Discuss these activities in a small group. Which activities seem to be purposeful? Which seem random?

- Find out how fast a mouse can run. First count the number of revolutions of the activity wheel the mouse makes in one minute. (Hint: Place a piece of masking tape on the rim of the activity wheel to make counting the revolutions easier.) Then multiply the number of revolutions times the circumference of the wheel. This will give you the distance the mouse can run per minute.

- If a balance or scale is available, weigh a mouse (or mice) once each week and record the data. After several weeks, graph the results to show any fluctuation in weight.

Rats

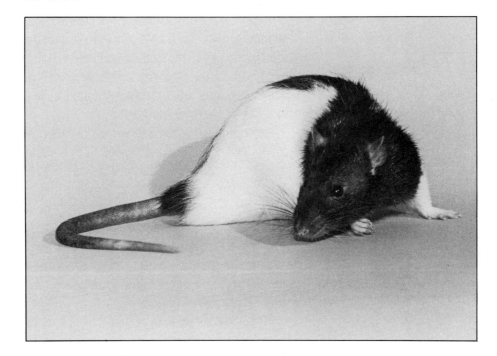

Background

Rats look like big mice and they have a similar natural history. But rats are, in fact, totally different animals. Rats are usually 7 to 10 inches (18–25 cm) in body length and some weigh over a pound (454 g). The familiar white rats are albino descendants of the wild Norway rat, which is also known by the more descriptive name, brown rat. Under domestication, a number of coat colors have been developed, and now white rats can be white, black, brown, tan, or any combination of these colors. Certain color combinations are so consistently produced that they warrant separate distinction. The hooded rat, for example, is all white with a black head.

Norway rats apparently originated in present-day Asia. Their arrival in Europe was relatively recent compared with the house mouse and the black rat, which arrived in the Middle Ages from southern Asia via the Mediterranean route. The black rat is a primary reservoir of the bubonic plague, and the disease is transmitted to humans by a flea that infests its fur. Following the arrival of the black rat, Europe suffered wave after wave of the Black Death and lost a quarter or more of its human population. The Norway rat and the black rat do not normally co-exist, and the larger Norway rat usually replaces the black rat when the two come together, at least in temperate climates. Thus the Norway rat could have played a major role in stopping the spread of the plague because, even though the Norway rat is a potential reservoir of the plague, the flea that transmits the disease is not normally one of its parasites. So, as destructive as Norway rats are, their arrival may have been a fortuitous event in the history of Europe.

From Europe, both kinds of rats were transported around the world along with the cargo in ships. The Norway rat seems to favor temperate climates and is the dominate species in those regions. The black rat is more adaptable and can thrive anywhere, but because of the aggressiveness of the Norway rat, it is largely confined to tropical and subtropical climates not inhabited by the Norway rat. Thus, with the exception of the polar areas, one rat species or the other is found in practically every part of the world that is occupied by humans.

Although rats can live alone in nature, they are much more likely to be associated with human activity. They occupy dwellings, barns, grain storage structures, factories, and sewers. They gain entry to these places by gnawing through walls or by digging under foundations. They are also inclined to dig and live in burrows, but these, too, are usually not far from human activity. Waste storage facilities, especially city dumps and landfills, are also favorite haunts for them. Rats are often associated with run-down areas of large cities where they sometimes live in abundance, but rats are not restricted by economic boundaries, and no place is immune to them if food is available.

Rats are difficult to count, but it is estimated that there are more rats than people on this planet. One of the reasons for their success is that they have the capacity to eat and thrive on virtually any food. They will eat any kind of food that humans eat; and if they don't get it before we do, they will eat the leftovers. This accounts for their attraction to stored food and exposed garbage and their abundance around disposal sites. They will also eat pet food, either from the bag or out of the dish when Rover is not looking. On farms they will eat stored grain and eggs and have even been known to kill and eat chickens and baby pigs.

Reproduction

Another reason for the success of rats is their great capacity to reproduce. A female can produce a litter of young about every 30 days throughout the 12 to 14 months of her reproductive life. The average litter size is 6 to 10, although as many as 20 can be born at once. The young reach reproductive age in about three months and, with a short gestation period of about three weeks, can be nursing young of their own by the age of four months. Meanwhile, the original mother could have produced at least four more litters and there would be a total of 48 rats. (This assumes an average litter of eight, half of which are females, and that they all survive.) One source suggests that, under ideal conditions, the descendants of a single pair of rats could theoretically total 20 million in three years.

Destruction of Food

Wherever they occur, rats can cause a great deal of economic loss and human suffering. Grain seems to be especially appealing to them, and great measures must be taken to protect it wherever it is stored. Not all grain receives the needed protection, though, and it is estimated that enough is lost to rats alone to eliminate hunger throughout the world. Unfortunately, a considerable amount of food that is not eaten is fouled by rat feces and urine. Large amounts of processed food are similarly destroyed in warehouses and kitchen cupboards. In gaining access to buildings, rats sometimes cause a great deal of physical damage by gnawing holes through walls and undermining foundations. They have also been implicated in causing fires by gnawing through electrical wiring.

Transmission of Diseases

Rats are also notorious for their role in the transmission of diseases. Mention has already been made of the importance of the black rat in spreading the Black Death through Europe. Rats are also implicated in carrying the causative agents of salmonellosis, rabies, trichinosis, ratbite fever, and various forms of typhus. These diseases may be transmitted to humans through rat bites, through the consumption of food contaminated with rat feces or urine, and through bites from fleas that have fed on rats.

Contributions to Research

Like mice, rats have partially redeemed themselves by serving as experimental animals. Much of our understanding of human physiology is based on studies of rats. They have been used extensively in studies on nutrition, heredity, endocrinology, organ transplants, drugs, cancer, and disease transmission. Practically no area of human physiology has remained unaffected by studies of rats, but rat research is not confined to biology. Sociologists have studied the interaction and population dynamics of rats under various conditions, and psychologists have used them in numerous studies of learning and behavior.

Rats in the Classroom

Unlike their wild relatives, laboratory rats are quite docile and easy to handle if they receive regular attention. In fact, they are less likely to bite than most other rodents. Their size and relatively slow movements make them easy to pick up and hold. They are quiet and if kept clean do not have a very objectionable odor. Rats eat and drink almost continuously, so food and water should be available at all times. They defecate and urinate just as frequently , so their cage needs cleaning two or three times each week. Probably their most undesirable characteristic is that they are inclined to defecate and sometimes urinate while being held. This problem can be reduced if they are handled only for short periods of time.

How to Obtain

Rats are sometimes available at local pet stores but less commonly so than other small mammals such as mice, gerbils, hamsters, and guinea pigs. It might be possible to obtain rats from a private individual—perhaps a student. They are also available from some biological supply companies (see Resources, page 226).

Caring for Rats

Housing   Rats can be kept in a variety of cages. Because of its convenience, a rat-sized commercial rodent cage is ideal for an individual rat or a breeding pair. A 15-gallon (or larger) aquarium is also satisfactory if it has a secure screen top. A multipurpose mammal cage (as shown in Figures 2-7 and 2-8 on page 19) is suitable, especially if it has a screen bottom. A cage with a floor space of at least 18 by 18 inches (45 x 45 cm) or the equivalent area is adequate for a pair of rats. If a cage with a solid bottom is used, an inch or two (2.5–5 cm) of wood shavings or cat litter should be added to

Rat in a commercial rodent cage

absorb moisture and help eliminate odor. Two or three shredded paper towels should be provided so that the rat can build a nest. Because of the frequency of waste elimination, a cage with a wire screen bottom is often recommended to prevent the rat from tracking through the waste material. If this type of cage is used, several thicknesses of newspaper can be placed under the screen to catch the wastes. In this case, cleaning the cage involves only replacing the newspaper. A nest box or bowl should be provided so that the rat does not have to stand or lie on the screen continuously. The nest normally will not be fouled with waste if it is just large enough for the occupant. Also, a piece of wood should be placed in the cage so the rat can gnaw on it if it chooses to do so.

Diet   Food and water should be available on a continuous basis. Commercial rat or rodent chow will ensure an adequate diet. This can be supplemented with canned or dry dog food and a variety of plant matter, such as carrots, apples, potatoes, and lettuce. Rats are less likely than mice to foul their food, so it can be provided in a heavy bowl. However, it is better to place the food in a suspended wire basket or a gravity-flow food hopper where an adequate supply can be held and where cleanliness is assured. Older rats will sometimes become obese. This is difficult to prevent because rats are adapted to feeding on a continuous basis and should have the opportunity to do so even if it appears that they are eating too much. Water should be provided in an inverted water bottle, which should be rinsed and refilled frequently. If an adequate supply of food and water is provided, rats can be left unattended over weekends. For longer periods, some arrangements will need to be made for the animals' care.

A Note on Handling

To pick up a rat, place the fingers of one hand under the rat's chest, with the index finger ahead of the foreleg and the thumb over the back. Then simply raise the animal and support it with the other hand.

Breeding Rats

Rats will readily reproduce under classroom conditions. A breeding pair can be kept in any of the standard cages. If nesting material is available to them, no additional preparation is necessary other than normal day-to-day care. When selecting rats for breeding purposes, it is best to obtain two that are about the same age. It is fairly easy to determine their sex because the testes of males are large and prominent at the base of the tail. Mating normally occurs within a few days if the pair is mature. Some books recommend removing the male before the young are born. This is not really necessary unless the growing litter causes crowded conditions or if one wishes to prevent the adults from mating again immediately. The gestation and maturation periods are very short. The young are born 21 to 22 days after mating. Hair appears after about one week and the eyes open in about 12 days. They are weaned at 20 to 25 days and reach sexual maturity at three months. After weaning, the young should be separated from the parents, and before the onset of maturity, the young males and females should be separated. (See also *A Special Note on Animal Reproduction,* page 186.)

When the Project Is Over

See page 10 in Chapter 1 for suggestions on what to do with animals that are no longer wanted or needed in the classroom.

Observations, Activities, and Questions

- Observe and describe a rat. Does it have whiskers? Does it have hair on its ears? Does it have hair on its tail? What color are its eyes?

- Record everything a rat does in a certain period of time. Discuss these activities in a small group. Which activities seem to be purposeful? Which seem random?

- If a balance or scale is available, weigh the rat (or rats) once each week and record the data. After several weeks, graph the results to show any fluctuation in weight.

Gerbils

Background

Gerbils are fairly new to the pet scene in North America; but since they were introduced to this continent in the 1950s, they have become well-known and are popular classroom pets. These rodents are midway in size between mice and rats, with a typical adult being about 4½ to 5 inches (11–12.5 cm) in body length and having a somewhat shorter tail, which is covered with short hair. At maturity, their weight is approximately three ounces (85 g). In nature, gerbils are typically sandy-brown in color, and this is the most familiar color of pet gerbils. However, other colors such as black, white, and tan have been produced through selective breeding.

Gerbils are native to the deserts and dry areas of Asia, Africa, and Eastern Europe. They are primarily nocturnal, preferring to spend the daytime hours in their underground burrows and are thus not regularly seen. They are most active at night when they come to the surface to search for the seeds, leaves, and other plant parts that they use for food and nest material. Some of the food is eaten immediately, but large amounts of it are stored in underground chambers for future use.

Adaptations

Like most other desert mammals, gerbils have several interesting behavioral and physiological adaptations for survival in their harsh environment. First, they have adjusted to living with very little water intake, and they can obtain most of their moisture needs from their food. Second, they have both behavioral and physiological adaptations to prevent water loss. Most mammals lose water in two ways: through breathing and through waste elimination. Gerbils are very conservative in both of these habits. Their fecal pellets are very dry and they give off very little urine. Also, by being nocturnal, gerbils do more than avoid hot temperatures. It is a simple physical fact that given a certain amount of moisture in the air, the cooler the temperature becomes, the higher the relative humidity will be. And, breathing dry air causes greater water loss than breathing moist air. Thus, by being nocturnal, gerbils lose considerably less water by breathing the cool and relatively moist nighttime desert air.

Common Misconceptions

The adaptations of gerbils for living in desert conditions have led to two rather common misconceptions about their care as pets. One is that they do not drink water or that they can go for months without it because, in theory, they can get what they need from their food. The other misconception is that their cages never need cleaning. Both of these perceptions have some biological basis, but both are, in fact, inaccurate and can lead to improper care. It is true that in nature gerbils drink very little, if any, water but in nature they can select foods that provide for their moisture needs, such as succulent leaves. The dry seeds, dry dog food, and pelletized rodent food that are often recommended for gerbils contain very little water and these foods alone will not meet their moisture needs. With a proper diet, consisting of these dry foods supplemented regularly with a variety of vegetables, gerbils can survive for long periods, perhaps throughout their lives (however long), without drinking water. However, if too little fluid is consumed as a result of an inadequate diet, physiological stress, reduced reproduction, and higher mortality can occur. Given all these considerations, it is better to give gerbils a source of water and let them have a drink if they desire it.

The idea that gerbil cages do not need to be cleaned is related to the misconception about water consumption—if gerbils do not drink, they will not urinate and therefore they will not smell. It is true that gerbils urinate very little and they are practically odor free. But any animal that consumes food will eliminate wastes. Since gerbils continually dig and stir their litter, the wastes become incorporated and are less visible, but they are there. Gerbils deserve to have a clean, healthy environment, so their cages should be cleaned at least once a week.

Gerbils in the Classroom

The popularity of gerbils as classroom animals can be attributed to several qualities. Being relatively small, they do not require very much space. If handled regularly, they become quite docile. They are quiet, practically odor free, not especially susceptible to diseases, and easy to care for. This combination of characteristics makes gerbils especially good animals to keep in the classroom.

How to Obtain

Gerbils are often available at local pet shops. Because of their popularity as pets, it might also be possible to obtain gerbils from a private individual—perhaps a student. In any case, be sure to select ones that appear alert and healthy. Gerbils are also available from some biological supply companies. See Resources, page 226. (Note: Some states with natural deserts prohibit the importation of gerbils. Check with your state's wildlife agency for information. See page 227 for the address.)

Caring for Gerbils

Housing   Gerbils are adaptable and can be kept in a variety of cages. The screen-covered aquarium (Figure 2-6), the commercial rodent cage (Figure 2-10), and the multipurpose mammal cages (Figures 2-7, 2-8, and 2-9) described in Chapter 2 are all satisfactory. Gerbils are active animals and should be given plenty of space. A pair can be kept in a 10-gallon aquarium, but a larger one is more desirable. A floor space of 1 by 2 feet (30 x 60 cm) is recommended for a pair of gerbils.

Gerbils in commercial gerbil cage

Several ingenious kinds of cages have been designed especially for gerbils and are available from pet stores. Some of them have rooms on different levels with ladders and passageways. Some even have a system of clear plastic tubes through which the gerbils can crawl from chamber to chamber. There is room for lots of ingenuity in designing gerbil cages. Although gerbils can climb, they can barely jump, so they can be kept in an open container if the sides are smooth to prevent them from climbing out. As a result, they have even been kept in such containers as an old bathtub and a livestock water tank. But whatever cage one selects, it should have a solid bottom to prevent the food and cage litter from falling through. Two or more inches (5 cm) of wood shavings or commercial cat litter can be used as a substrate, and this should be changed every week. If a few paper towels, tubes from paper towel rolls, or pieces of cardboard are placed in the cage, the gerbils will quickly shred them to create more litter, which they seem to enjoy doing. A piece of wood can also be added to the cage for the gerbils to gnaw on if they wish.

Gerbils are very active animals and will utilize an exercise wheel as much as or more than any of the other classroom mammals. An exercise wheel with a revolution counter has been used to determine that a pair of gerbils can run an average of three to five miles in a 24-hour period.

Diet   Gerbils will eat many kinds of seeds, including barley, corn, oats, and wheat, but sunflower seeds seem to be their favorite. Most pet stores sell a gerbil food mix that contains a variety of seeds and sometimes pelleted hay. The wild bird seed that is available in most grocery stores is also an excellent food for gerbils. Gerbils can also be fed the pelleted natural-ingredient foods for rats, guinea pigs, mice, or rabbits in place of or in addition to a seed mixture. In order to ensure an adequate diet, gerbils should be fed a variety of foods, including green leafy vegetables or succulent fruits and vegetables. Pieces of celery, carrot, lettuce, and apple and other fruits will be readily accepted and should be offered at least twice each week.

Gerbils have a natural tendency to hoard food, and this makes it difficult to determine the best amount to feed them. They will not overeat, but after consuming what they want, they will hide the rest somewhere in their cage, usually mixed with the litter. This makes a gravity-flow food hopper impractical because it will quickly be emptied, and the food will be moved elsewhere. A food dish is emptied just as quickly or is otherwise filled with litter, but this is probably the best way to feed gerbils because you can control the amount of food in the dish. An adult will consume two to three teaspoons of seeds each day, but this amount will vary from specimen to specimen. The best thing to do is to give them a certain amount of food on a regular basis and then adjust the amount as needed. Food that has been hoarded will eventually be consumed if it is not discarded with the litter when the cage is cleaned.

As mentioned earlier, gerbils should always have the opportunity to drink water if they desire it. Considering the tendency of gerbils to fill any container with cage litter, though, a water dish is not suitable. The only practical way to provide water for them is with an inverted water bottle. If an adequate supply of food and water is provided, gerbils can be left for weekends without further attention. For longer periods, some arrangements will need to be made for the animals' care.

A Note on Handling

Gerbils are skittish animals and are sometimes difficult to pick up, especially if they are not accustomed to it. Even when being held, they will often struggle and attempt to jump free. But a gerbil can be picked up, and the process can be simplified by first gaining its confidence. To do so, offer the gerbil food regularly from the hand and allow it to sniff and investigate. Then, place one hand around the body and place the other hand under its feet. Or cup both hands around it, with the fingers slightly apart to form a cage. Hold it only briefly at first and always be prepared to return it to the cage quickly if it begins to struggle. If it is necessary to pick up a gerbil before this comfort level is achieved, simply place a jar or can over it and then slide one hand or a piece of cardboard under the container to confine it. A word of caution: Never attempt to pick up a gerbil by the tail.

Breeding Gerbils

A male and a female gerbil might not be immediately compatible when placed together, so several attempts might have to be made to mate them. However, like rats and mice, once mated, a pair of gerbils can be kept together indefinitely. They will mate in their own time and raise their young without requiring special attention or concern. In fact, the appearance of baby gerbils is often a surprise because adult females tend to show few signs of pregnancy. Gestation in gerbils is 24 to 25 days. The litter size ranges from one to ten, but the most common litter size is four or five. Newborn gerbils are about an inch (2.5 cm) in length. They are pink and hairless, and their eyes are closed. After a few days, they begin growing light-colored hair and are able to crawl around the nest. By two weeks, they have a new coat of darker hair, have grown considerably, and are able to leave the nest to investigate the cage. At this time, their eyes are not yet open, but they have already developed the inquisitive nature characteristic of older gerbils. In a few more days, their eyes open and they can move freely around the cage. At about 30 days, the young can be weaned and placed in a separate cage until just before they reach sexual maturity. (See also *A Special Note on Animal Reproduction,* page 186.)

Gerbils reach sexual maturity in 10 to 12 weeks and fertility lasts until they are 12 to 18 months old. In this time, it is possible for a single pair to produce 8 to 12 litters. The life span of a gerbil is typically three to four years, but occasionally specimens live more than five years.

When the Project Is Over

See page 10 in Chapter 1 for suggestions on what to do with animals that are no longer wanted or needed in the classroom.

Observations, Activities, and Questions

- Observe and describe a gerbil. Does it have whiskers? Does it have hair on its ears? Does it have hair on its tail? What color are its eyes?

- Record everything a gerbil does in a certain period of time. Discuss these activities in a small group. Which activities seem to be purposeful? Which seem random?

- Find out how fast a gerbil can run. First, count the number of revolutions of the activity wheel the gerbil makes in one minute. (Hint: Place a piece of masking tape on the rim of the activity wheel to make counting the revolutions easier.) Then multiply the number of revolutions times the circumference of the wheel. This will give you the distance the gerbil can run per minute.

- If a balance or scale is available, weigh the gerbil (or gerbils) once each week and record the data. After several weeks, graph the results to show any fluctuation in weight.

Hamsters

Hamsters are small, plump, short-legged, stubby-tailed rodents. At maturity, they are about 5 inches (12.5 cm) long and weigh from 4 to 5 ounces (112–140 g). The natural color of hamsters is reddish-gold with white underparts. However, selective breeding of hamsters with color mutations has resulted in various colors, such as cinnamon, white, cream, and gray, and these colors can be either spotted or solid. Hamsters have loose skin, large cheek pouches, prominent black eyes, and large upright ears, giving them a very appealing appearance. However, their appearance is sometimes deceiving. Although they are normally friendly, hamsters can be pugnacious, and they have the teeth to back up their attitude. But for the most part, they are friendly and make desirable pets.

Several kinds of hamsters occur in Europe and Asia, but the type that is usually kept as a pet is the golden hamster. This species was formerly known as the Syrian hamster because it was first captured in Syria in 1930. It is hard to believe that such an animal could have been virtually unknown until this late date, but because of its secretive habits, the golden hamster is seldom seen in nature. It was fortuitous that a scientist got a glimpse of an animal that he could not identify as it entered its burrow. His curiosity caused him to excavate the burrow to find the animal. Eight feet (2.4 m) underground he succeeded in capturing the first known golden hamsters— a female, with 12 young. The family was taken to a laboratory where a colony was established; from there, hamsters were transported around the world. The initial interest in hamsters was for scientific curiosity and, later, for research. The first hamsters arrived in the United States in 1938 via London. It is interesting to note that virtually all of the thousands of golden hamsters that have been kept as pets and used in research are descendants of that original family that was captured in 1930.

As for their life in the wild, it is now known that hamsters live in deep burrows that usually have several sleeping rooms and chambers for food storage. They are nocturnal and come to the surface at night to gather seeds, which they carry in their cheek pouches and hoard in massive amounts in the underground chambers. Since much of their food consists of grain, hamsters can cause considerable damage to crops. They hibernate during cooler months but awaken frequently to feed on the stored food. Otherwise, the details of their life in nature are not well known or have been inferred from observing them in captivity.

Reproduction

Apart from their appearance and the story of their discovery, one of the more interesting things about golden hamsters is their high reproductive potential. The gestation period of hamsters—only 16 days—is one of the shortest of all mammals. They also have a very short maturation period, requiring only about one month before they reach sexual maturity. They also tend to have fairly large litters of 7 to 10, with as many as 15 being possible. Considering all of these factors, it is theoretically possible for a single pair of hamsters and their offspring to produce thousands of hamsters in one year. At the same time, hamsters have a fairly short life span and typically live only a year or two. During this time, females usually produce six to nine litters.

Hamsters in the Classroom

Since their introduction and growth in popularity as pets, golden hamsters have been kept successfully in thousands of classrooms. As classroom animals, hamsters have some excellent attributes. They are so quiet that their presence will rarely be noticed. Further, they are clean, virtually odor free, and are as easy, or easier, to care for as any of the other laboratory mammals. No animal is perfect, though, and even hamsters have some negative qualities. They are more likely than other classroom mammals to bite, and they can do so with vehemence. (Any bite should, of course, receive prompt medical attention.) However, if handled regularly, most hamsters are generally docile. They do seem to recognize their keeper, though, and are sometimes alarmed by strangers. As a result, they might not respond well to students taking turns caring for them.

Hamsters are also the most strongly nocturnal of the laboratory mammals and if left undisturbed will be active only at night and rarely seen during the day. This has several consequences. First, it accounts for their being a little grumpy at times. For a hamster to be awakened during the day is akin to a person being awakened at night, and this does not always bring out one's most favorable qualities. It also means that students will not be able to observe most of the hamster's routine activities.

How to Obtain

Hamsters are often available at local pet shops. Because of their popularity as pets, it might also be possible to obtain hamsters from a private individual—perhaps a student. In any case, be sure to select ones that appear alert and healthy. Hamsters are also available from some biological supply companies (see Resources, page 226).

Caring for Hamsters

Housing   Hamsters can be kept in a variety of cages, including a screen-covered aquarium, a commercial rodent cage, or a multipurpose mammal cage. (These cages are described and illustrated on pages 18–20.) Wooden cages or any other cages that the hamsters can gnaw need to be covered on the inside with wire screen. The floor space of the cage should measure at least 12 by 24 inches (30 x 60 cm) for a pair of hamsters and their young. Hamsters are inclined to hoard food in corners, among litter, or in the nest,

Hamster in a screen-covered aquarium

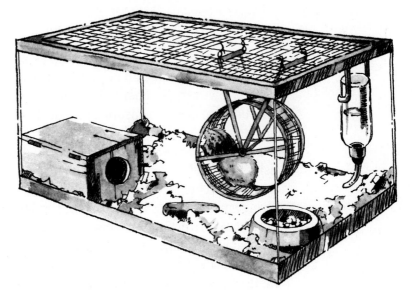

so if a cage with a wire screen bottom is used, much of the food could be lost. However, this problem can be avoided if the wire floor of the cage is covered with a piece of galvanized metal, wood, or hard plastic.

The cage floor should be covered with wood shavings, dry grass or hay, shredded paper towels, or commercial pet litter to a depth of 1 to 2 inches (2.5–5 cm). A wooden block for gnawing and an activity wheel should also be added to the cage.

Because of their nocturnal habits and apparent desire for seclusion, hamsters should be provided with a wooden or cardboard nest box with a 2- to 3-inch (5–7.5 cm) diameter entrance hole in the center of one side. The top should be hinged or at least be easy to remove. The nest box will be gnawed and eventually will have to be replaced, but it will meet the hamsters' needs.

The hamsters will spend most of their time in the nest box, so it will have to be opened to observe them. Open it gently and reach in with care; this is home to the hamsters, and they sometimes show a tendency to defend it. If nest materials, such as dried grass, straw, shredded paper towels, or pieces of cloth are available, the hamsters will fill the box and keep it clean. If two nest boxes are provided, the hamsters are likely to use one for sleeping and one for food storage.

Hamsters are fastidious and will treat their cage like an underground tunnel, using part of it for nesting (the nest box) and part of it for food storage (selected corners or a second nest box). They will also consistently select a certain area of the cage to eliminate their waste. This organization seems to be an integral part of their needs. These factors should be considered when cleaning the cage. If all the litter is simply dumped out, as is done with other rodents, part of the hamsters' organized home will be destroyed. It is better to identify the part of the cage used for waste elimination and simply scoop out and replace that portion of litter. This needs to be done only once a week.

Diet   Hamsters will consume a wide variety of foods, including seeds, raw vegetables, nuts, and fruits such as apples and raisins. Occasionally, they will also consume an insect, such as a cricket, grasshopper, or mealworm. However, commercially prepared rodent pellets should be available at all times in order to ensure an adequate diet. A mixture of about one-half hamster pellets and one-half wild bird seed provides a well-balanced and varied diet. Hamsters do not foul their food, so it can be provided in a heavy dish. They will not overeat, but no matter how much food is offered, the hamsters will empty the dish and hide the uneaten portion. To store food during times of plenty is a part of the hamster's natural behavior. This cushion against hard times seems to be a comfort to hamsters (like having money in the bank), so it is best to allow them to store a little food.

As basically dry land animals, hamsters do not consume much water, but they will take some, and it should be available at all times. Water is best provided with an inverted water bottle, which should be rinsed and refilled frequently. If left with an adequate supply of food and water, hamsters can be left unattended over weekends. For longer periods, some arrangements will need to be made for the animals' care.

A Note on Handling

Being slow moving and more inclined to sit quietly than most small mammals, hamsters are easy to pick up and hold. Approach a hamster slowly, however, and if it seems reluctant, gain its confidence by offering it food in your hand. If the hamster is asleep, awaken it gently before attempting to pick it up. Then, pick it up with both hands cupped around its body; or pick it up with one hand by placing the fingers around the body and the thumb over the shoulders. In either case, great care should be exercised to prevent the hamster from falling.

Breeding Hamsters

Like other laboratory animals, hamsters will reproduce in the classroom, but they are much more temperamental about it. Since hamsters are possessive and protective of their cages, just placing a member of the opposite sex into a hamster's cage can result in some disenchantment. If any sign of aggression occurs, immediately remove the original occupant and allow the other to explore the cage for a few minutes. Then reintroduce the two. Watch them carefully for at least 15 minutes and then check them periodically for several hours. A certain amount of nipping and fussing seems to be a part of normal hamster interaction (play); but if any sign of aggressive behavior occurs, they should again be separated. This might not resolve the differences, but another attempt to mate them a few days later might be successful. If three or four attempts to mate two hamsters are unsuccessful, they should be considered incompatible and not be reintroduced.

When it becomes obvious that the female is pregnant, it is best to remove the male from the cage. The female should not be disturbed any more than necessary until a week or two after the young are born. Hamsters are more inclined to kill and consume their young than other mammals. Removing the male will help reduce the problem, but since the female may also eat them, she and the young should not be disturbed.

The female will be receptive again within a few days after giving birth, but it is best not to allow the pair to mate again until after the young are weaned. After weaning, the young males and females should be separated, since they reach sexual maturity at about one month of age. It is best not to breed the young until they are about three or four months old. The juvenile females can be kept together, but the males will require separate housing to prevent aggressive behavior. After weaning, the young can be fed and cared for in the same manner as the adults. (See also *A Special Note on Animal Reproduction,* page 186.)

When the Project Is Over

See page 10 in Chapter 1 for suggestions on what to do with animals that are no longer wanted or needed in the classroom.

Observations, Activities, and Questions

• Observe and describe a hamster. Does it have whiskers? Does it have hair on its ears? Does it have hair on its tail? What color are its eyes?

• Record everything a hamster does in a certain period of time. Discuss these activities in a small group. Which activities seem to be purposeful? Which seem random?

• Find out how many sunflower seeds a hamster can hold in its cheek pouches. Place one hundred sunflower seeds in the hamster's food container and watch it fill its pouches. Then remove the food container and count the remaining seeds.

• Find out how fast a hamster can run. First, count the number of revolutions of the activity wheel the hamster makes in one minute. (Hint: Place a piece of masking tape on the rim of the activity wheel to make counting the revolutions easier.) Then multiply the number of revolutions times the circumference of the wheel. This will give you the distance the hamster can run per minute.

• If a balance or scale is available, weigh a hamster (or hamsters) once each week and record the data. After several weeks, graph the results to show any fluctuation in weight.

Guinea Pigs

Background

The name *guinea pig* is a curious one because this animal is a rodent, not a pig, and it does not come from Guinea. Guinea pig fanciers who raise them for competitive shows like to call them *cavies*, a name derived from their scientific name, *Cavia porcellus*. Guinea pigs are native to the high mountains of Peru, where they live in shallow burrows or rock crevices and feed on practically any available vegetation. They were domesticated by the Incas centuries ago, probably for use as a food source, and they continue to be used for this purpose today. From Peru, guinea pigs were transported around the world, not as stowaways, as was the case of mice and rats, but probably as a food source on early sailing vessels.

Characteristics

Because guinea pigs have been domesticated for centuries, they no longer closely resemble their larger, brown, wild ancestors, Today's pet guinea pigs vary in length from 8 to 12 inches (20–30 cm) and weigh about 1 pound (0.5 kg). They have a short, plump body and legs that are so short that they can neither jump nor climb. Their eyes are large and set close together and their rounded ears are hairless. A variety of colors and coat types have been developed through selective breeding of domestic stock. Guinea pigs can be solid white, black, brown, tan, red, or any combination of these colors. Coat types are distinctive and have separate names. The English guinea pig has a short, smooth coat; the Abyssinian or rough guinea pig has slightly longer hair that grows in swirls or rosettes over the body; and the Peruvian or Angora guinea pig has extremely long hair, sometimes as long as 6 inches (15 cm). Guinea pig fanciers use special names for the various combinations of colors and hair types.

Guinea pigs are also bred extensively for use as experimental animals. They have played an important role in the development of many drugs and have also been used in studies of behavior, heredity, and nutrition.

Reproduction

Compared with other rodents, guinea pig reproduction is unique in two major ways. First, the gestation period of 60 to 70 days is unusually long. Second, the young are well developed at birth and mature quickly. They have a full coat of hair and a full set of adult teeth, their eyes open immediately, and they can run about within minutes after birth. They also begin consuming solid food almost immediately and may be weaned in as few as ten days. They grow rapidly, and the young females can conceive at less than one month of age. The degree of development at birth is interesting and the rapid maturation may seem astounding, but both of these phenomena are a function of the long gestation period. Both seem less unusual if one measures the time of development from conception to maturity rather than from birth to maturity. The total time is then about three and one-half months for guinea pigs. Rats, with a short gestation period and a longer immature period, have a total development time of less than four months, which is not much longer than guinea pigs. Mice, with both a short gestation period and short immature stage, have a total development period of three months. Perhaps guinea pigs are not so unique in this respect after all. Motherhood is just a matter of style; the outcome is about the same.

Another effect, though, of the long gestation period is that the reproductive potential is greatly reduced. Since each pregnancy lasts for over two months, a female cannot produce more than five litters in year. Then, too, because the young are large at the time of birth, the litter size is smaller. The female simply cannot carry the larger number that is typical of other rodents. The litters range from one to five (rarely six), but the average number is about three. On the average, a female produces 12 to 15 young each year. This lower productivity is partially made up for by longer periods of fertility and a longer life span—females can reproduce for two to three years, and guinea pigs can live to be ten years old, although their lives are usually shorter.

Guinea Pigs in the Classroom

Because of their docile nature, guinea pigs are ideal mammals to keep in the classroom. Their size makes them easy to pick up and hold, even by little hands. They are especially tolerant of being handled and rarely bite. They consume a relatively large amount of food and water for their size and, consequently, produce copious amounts of droppings and urine. These wastes do not have the objectionable odor so characteristic of mice, though, and if the cage is cleaned regularly, it is not a major problem. Guinea pigs are more vocal than other rodents, but this is usually limited to an occasional squeal (in apparent delight) when they are fed or placed in a clean cage.

How to Obtain

Guinea pigs are often available at local pet shops. Because of their popularity, it might also be possible to obtain a guinea pig from a private individual—perhaps a student. In any case, be sure to select one that appears alert and healthy.

Caring for Guinea Pigs

Housing   The fact that guinea pigs cannot climb or jump allows for more flexibility in housing them than is the case with most other rodents. But since guinea pigs are relatively large, they require slightly more space than smaller mammals. A standard 15- or 20-gallon aquarium, a multipurpose mammal cage (see Figures 2-7 and 2-8 on page 19), or even a large wooden box will make a suitable enclosure. If the sides of the container are about one foot (30 cm) high, a cover is not needed, since the guinea pigs will not be able to climb out. If an individual guinea pig is being kept, the cage should have a floor space of at least 24 by 36 inches (60-90 cm). If two or more are kept, the cage should have at least 4 square feet (0.36 m^2) of floor space for each animal. Although not necessary, guinea pigs will utilize a shallow nest box, but it should be heavy enough that it will not tip over. If a cage with a solid bottom is used, the floor should be covered with 1 to 2 inches (2.5–5 cm) of wood shavings or cat litter. The litter should be changed at least once each week or as needed to provide a dry, sanitary environment. If a cage with a screen bottom is used, several thicknesses of newspaper placed below the screen will absorb the urine and catch the

Guinea pig in a large wooden box

droppings. In this case, cleaning the cage involves only changing the paper. Although guinea pigs are not inclined to gnaw as much as some rodents, they should have a piece of wood to gnaw on if they wish to do so. Also, they do not use an activity wheel.

Assuming that the cage is large enough, several females can be housed together, or several females can be kept with a single male. However, if several females are kept together, they tend to become cliquish and will sometimes not accept a new female cage mate. One solution to this problem is to remove the original residents and place the new female in the cage for an hour or two. Then return the original occupants, one at a time, so that they will gradually become acquainted. Two or more mature males are usually incompatible and, even if they appear to get along, should not be housed together because a fight might ensue.

Diet   Guinea pigs usually consume only a small amount of food and water at a time, but they eat and drink frequently, and during the course of a day, their total intake is fairly high for an animal of their size. Food and water should, therefore, be available at all times. Although they are strictly vegetarian, guinea pigs are otherwise not fussy about their diet and will accept practically any type of plant material, including seeds, raw vegetables, and fruits. They will also consume grass, clover, dandelion leaves, and hay if it is available. However, guinea pigs, like humans, require a small amount of vitamin C on a regular basis, so fortified commercial guinea pig food should be the staple diet, supplemented with any of the foods previously mentioned.

If possible, the food should be provided in a gravity-flow food hopper suspended above the cage floor to prevent fouling and to provide a continuous supply of food. If a food dish is used, it should be heavy enough to prevent tipping and, to reduce contamination, small enough that the animals cannot climb into it. There may still be some fouling of the food if a dish is used, so the hopper-style feeder is strongly recommended, especially if the animals will be unattended over weekends.

Water is most conveniently provided with an inverted water bottle. Because of the relatively large amount of water consumed, a bottle of at least one-half liter should be used. For weekends, two or more water bottles might be needed. This can be determined by monitoring the daily water consumption and planning accordingly.

A Note on Handling

Guinea pigs are often rather skittish about being picked up, but once used to being handled, they are usually docile. Grasp a guinea pig under the chest with three fingers behind and the index finger ahead of the foreleg and the thumb over the back. Then raise the guinea pig slightly and slide the palm of the free hand under it for support. Be cautious and do not let it fall.

Breeding Guinea Pigs

A breeding pair of guinea pigs should be kept in a cage with at least 8 square feet (0.72 m^2) of floor space and cared for as described above. Otherwise, no special preparations need to be made for reproduction. Mating will normally occur within a few days after the pair is placed together. Subsequent mating will occur within a few hours after the young are born if the male is allowed to remain with the female at the time of birth. It is best to separate the pair until after the young are weaned and have been removed from the cage. Otherwise, because of the very short maturation period, the adult male will mate with the young females. The young males and females should also be housed separately following weaning. Although female guinea pigs can conceive at about 30 days of age, they should not be bred until they are four or five months old, as early pregnancy is detrimental to their health. (See also *A Special Note on Animal Reproduction,* page 186.)

When the Project Is Over

See page 10 in Chapter 1 for suggestions on what to do with animals that are no longer wanted or needed in the classroom.

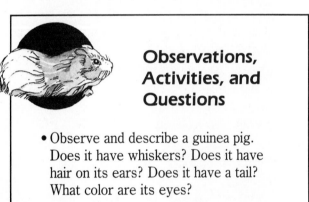

Observations, Activities, and Questions

- Observe and describe a guinea pig. Does it have whiskers? Does it have hair on its ears? Does it have a tail? What color are its eyes?

- Record everything a guinea pig does in a certain period of time. Discuss these activities in a small group. Which activities seem to be purposeful? Which seem random?

- If a balance or scale is available, weigh the guinea pig (or pigs) once each week and record the data. After several weeks, graph the results to show any fluctuation in weight.

Rabbits

Background

Rabbits, and their close relative, hares, are native to all the major continents and, as a group, have adapted to a wide variety of habitats. Their distribution in North America illustrates this point. The desert cottontail and the black-tailed jack rabbit are found in the deserts of the American southwest, the mountain cottontail in the western mountains, the eastern cottontail in the eastern hardwood forests, the white-tailed jack rabbit in the Great Plains, the snowshoe hare in the northern coniferous forests, and the Arctic hare in the tundra. Almost all parts of North America have one or more species of rabbits or hares, and this is true of other continents as well.

Characteristics

Most people are familiar with one member of the rabbit family or another. As a group, rabbits have soft hair, a short fluffy tail, relatively long ears, and disproportionately long hind legs. They often sit in a crouched position, which gives them a plump appearance, but when they stretch out to run, they are rather slender and agile. Hares are larger than rabbits, with adults reaching lengths of 22 inches (55 cm) and weighing up to 10 pounds (4.5 kg). The smallest member of the rabbit family is the pygmy rabbit, which reaches only 11 inches (27.5 cm) in length and one pound (.45 kg) in weight. The familiar cottontail reaches 17 inches (42.5 cm) in length and up to 4 pounds (1.8 kg) in weight.

At one time, rabbits and hares were classified, along with rats, mice, squirrels, beavers, and others, as rodents. More recently, scientists have decided that rabbits and hares are significantly different from rodents and have placed them in a separate category called *lagomorpha*. However, the difference between rabbits and hares is not obvious, and there is considerable confusion in their names. Jack rabbits and snowshoe rabbits, for example, are really hares, and the domestic Belgian hare is a rabbit. A primary distinction between hares and rabbits is that baby hares are *precocial*—they are born with a full coat of hair and open eyes, and they are able to run around within a few minutes of birth. Newborn rabbits, on the other hand, are *altricial*—they are blind, hairless, and virtually helpless. All domestic lagomorphs are true rabbits.

Wild rabbits and hares are usually some shade of brown or gray. In northern climates where winters are long and harsh, however, some kinds—such as the white-tailed jack rabbit, the snowshoe hare, and the Arctic hare—turn white during the winter months. This appears to be an obvious protective measure to make them less visible in the snow. However, changing colors is a gradual process. The stimulus that triggers the color change is not the arrival and disappearance of snow but rather the yearly shortening and lengthening of daylight hours.

Wild rabbits and hares have been introduced in many islands where, in the absence of predators, they have reproduced so prodigiously that they have become pests. This was especially true in Australia where, after being introduced in 1859, rabbits became so abundant that they competed with livestock for the sparse vegetation. All efforts to control their numbers failed until a rabbit disease called myxomatosis was introduced in the 1950s. This disease reduced and continues to control the rabbit population but has not eliminated it.

Cottontails

Because they commonly live in suburban areas, cottontails are probably the best known of the North American lagomorphs. They live in the protection of shrubs and gardens, where they sometimes make themselves unpopular because of their taste for vegetables. In a more natural setting, they seem to prefer thickets, brushy fence rows, and brush piles that are along open areas where they feed. They are vegetarians and consume a wide variety of green plants, including grass, clover, alfalfa, and, given the opportunity, lettuce and other vegetables.

Reproduction   Cottontails (as well as most other lagomorphs) are prolific. The gestation period is about 30 days, and a single female can produce as many as 6 litters each year, and each litter typically has 4 to 6 young. The nest consists of a shallow depression in the soil that is lined, for warmth, with hair that the female pulls from her abdomen. The young receive little parental attention other than frequent visits by the female to allow them to nurse. The young are weaned at about one month, and three to four months later they can produce young of their own. Before the end of the summer, a female and the young from two or three of her litters can all be producing young. If all the female's young survive to reproduce, a population explosion could ensue. But life is not easy for cottontails; they are preyed upon by a number of animals, including hawks, owls, foxes, weasels, and, in urban areas, cats. As with all other animals, the loss due to predation, disease, and old age is in balance with the rate of reproduction, so the population tends to remain stable.

Domesticated Rabbits

Rabbits have been kept in captivity for such a long time that the history of their domestication is not known. One account, however, suggests that European monks, who were not allowed to eat red meat, learned to raise rabbits for food, probably because rabbit flesh is so light-colored that it more closely resembles that of birds than mammals. Whatever their history, there are now sixty to eighty recognized varieties of domesticated rabbits, and all of them are thought to have originated from European rabbit stock.

Domesticated rabbits vary in size, coloration, and form, and each type has been given a distinct name. The small Netherland Dwarf, which weighs 2 to 3 pounds (0.9–1.4 kg) is not much larger than a guinea pig and is one of the smallest breeds. Other breeds range upward in size to the Flemish giant, which can be as large as 14 pounds (6.3 kg). The color of domesticated rabbits can be solid black, white, red, brown, tan, yellow, or gray, or combinations of these colors. The hair is typically short, but the hair of the Angora rabbit is long, fine, and luxuriant. Among the more unusual rabbits are the French and English lop-eared varieties, whose ears may reach a foot (30 cm) or more in length.

Today, domesticated rabbits are found almost worldwide and are kept for a number of reasons. They are an important source of food in many areas, especially in Europe, where they are readily available in markets. In the United States, rabbit meat is less popular, although many people raise rabbits for food in backyard hutches. Because of its warmth, rabbit fur is used to line hats and gloves. Rabbit fur is also used in the manufacture of felt cloth, and, of course, the soft Angora hair is spun into yarn for sweaters.

Rabbits are also used extensively in biological research and in the production and testing of vaccines. Finally, because they are docile and easy to care for, rabbits are kept extensively as pets.

Rabbits in the Classroom

Rabbits normally adjust well to the activity of a classroom. They can usually be handled with ease and can even be allowed occasionally to hop about the classroom, an event that is enjoyed by students. Rabbits consume quite a bit of food and thus produce a lot of droppings, but if the cage is cleaned daily, they do not have a very objectionable odor.

How to Obtain

Rabbits are sometimes available at local pet shops. Since rabbits are often kept as pets or raised for food, it is also possible to purchase one from a private individual. Watch for ads in a local newspaper. In any case, be sure to select a rabbit, preferably a female, that appears alert and healthy. Although any kind of rabbit is appropriate for the classroom, the smaller breeds are easier to house.

Caring for Rabbits

Housing   Being fairly large, rabbits require a larger cage than most other classroom animals. It is difficult to make a general statement about cage dimensions because adult rabbits vary so greatly in size. Generally, the smaller dwarf breeds should have a cage with a floor space of 2 by 3 feet (60 by 90 cm) when mature; larger breeds should have proportionally more floor space—not less than 2 by 4 feet (60 by 120 cm). The multipurpose cage shown here is an ideal design for rabbits. The front or side door will provide

Rabbit in a multipurpose wire cage

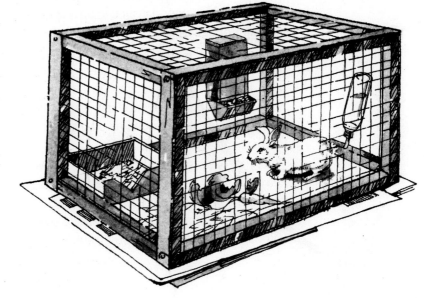

easy access for cleaning, and the wire screen bottom will allow droppings to fall through for easy removal. If a screen bottom cage is not available, the floor should be covered with 1 to 2 inches (2.5–5 cm) of wood shavings or commercial pet litter. In either case, the droppings should be removed daily for hygienic and aesthetic reasons. Most rabbits will utilize a nest box if available. If used, the nest box should be constructed of heavy material so that it will not tip over, and it should be partially filled with litter or straw. A 12 by 14-inch (30 by 35-cm) rectangular box about 6 to 8 inches (15–20 cm) high constructed of standard one-inch lumber is about right. A deep V-shaped notch cut in one end will make it more accessible, especially for young rabbits. Two or more juvenile rabbits can be kept in the same cage if it is large enough. After they reach maturity, however, rabbits will sometimes fight if kept together. Separate cages are required if more than one adult rabbit is kept.

Diet   As vegetarians, rabbits can be kept satisfactorily on a diet of mixed grains and hay. However, it is much easier to feed them commercial rabbit pellets (which are made of the same materials), and this can be supplemented with a variety of plant material, such as lettuce, cabbage, carrots, apples, an occasional handful of grass, and, if available, hay.

Rabbits have a curious habit of consuming their own droppings. This is related to their vegetarian diet. Because vegetation is hard to digest, rabbits can obtain more nutrition from food by passing it through the digestive system twice. Often when rabbits appear to be grooming, they are passing a pellet, which they immediately swallow.

In nature, rabbits seem to nibble continuously on some type of vegetation. They are accustomed to eating small amounts of food at a time, but in the course of a day, they generally consume a great deal. In keeping a pet rabbit, this should be taken into consideration, and in most cases, food should be available at all times. Nursing females and growing young especially should have food available on a continual basis. However, mature rabbits sometimes become obese. If this happens, feed them less of the more concentrated pellets—perhaps only the amount they will consume in a half hour in the morning and evening—but continue to give them some vegetable matter.

It is best to provide food in a gravity-flow food hopper attached to a wall of the cage. A heavy bowl or dish that cannot be tipped over is also satisfactory since rabbits are less inclined to foul their food than other animals. Water is best provided in an inverted water bottle, but if unavailable, a heavy dish is acceptable. In either case, the water container should be rinsed and refilled frequently. If provided with a sufficient supply of food and water, rabbits can be left unattended over weekends. For longer periods, some arrangements will need to be made for the animals' care.

A Note on Handling

A rabbit should never be picked up or held by the ears. The proper way to pick up a large rabbit is to grasp it firmly by the loose skin just above the shoulders with one hand; as it is raised up, place the other hand under the hind quarters for support. Once under control, most rabbits can be held in the arms, but care should be taken to prevent them from falling. A juvenile rabbit can be picked up by grasping it around the body with both hands. Students sometimes want to hold animals upside down, but this is an unnatural position and most rabbits, especially if they are not used to being handled, will struggle if held this way.

Breeding Rabbits

A mature female rabbit can conceive at any time and will normally mate within a few minutes after being placed with a male. She should then be returned to her cage and maintained as usual. Gestation is normally 31 to 32 days, and she should not be handled more than necessary during the last two weeks of the pregnancy. Of course, a nest box is necessary when young are expected.

When rabbits are born they are pink, hairless, and blind. Rabbits will tolerate some disturbance of their young, so the nest box can occasionally be removed from the cage for observation. The young will begin getting hair after about one week and their eyes will open at about two weeks. At this time they can safely be handled, but this should be done judiciously until they are older. The young can be weaned at six weeks, after which they should be cared for in the same manner as the adults. After weaning, the litter mates can be kept together if necessary, but since they reach sexual maturity in as few as five months, they should be separated before this time to prevent fighting and untimely and unwanted pregnancies. (See also *A Special Note on Animal Reproduction,* page 186.)

When the Project Is Over

See page 10 in Chapter 1 for suggestions on what to do with animals that are no longer wanted or needed in the classroom.

Observations, Activities, and Questions

- Observe and describe a rabbit. Does it have whiskers? What color are its eyes?

- Watch a rabbit eat. How does it use its lips to manipulate its food?

- Record everything a rabbit does in a certain period of time. Discuss these activities in a small group. Which activities seem to be purposeful? Which seem random?

- If a suitable balance or scale is available, weigh the rabbit (or rabbits) once each week and record the data. After several weeks, graph the results to show any fluctuation in weight.

Resources

The information in *Animals in the Classroom* will assist teachers in confidently maintaining a variety of animals in their classrooms. If the book's goal of stimulating interest in animals is achieved, however, both teachers and students will want additional information about animals and their lives. Because this type of information is available in a variety of forms from so many sources, no attempt has been made here to provide a comprehensive list of resources. Instead, types of resources are described, with examples in each category. Mention of specific books, magazines, companies, and organizations is not intended to imply endorsement but rather to provide examples of the many resources available to teachers.

Books

Animal books are an immediately available resource in most schools and libraries. They can be categorized according to their intended use.

General Books: Many excellent animal books for children and adults are readily available at school and public libraries and in bookstores. In addition to providing information, these books can help to foster positive attitudes toward animals. A valuable resource for selecting science books for children is *The AAAS Science Book List for Children,* published by the American Association for the Advancement of Science. This book is available at many libraries.

Animal Encyclopedias: Animal encyclopedias are usually single-volume, large-format books that present a survey of the animal kingdom or a certain group of animals. They are usually richly illustrated and include an overview of the natural history of selected animals from around the world. Examples of animal encyclopedias are:

Farrand, John, ed. ***The Audubon Society Encyclopedia of Animal Life.*** New York: Clarkson N. Potter, Inc., 1984.

Macmillan Illustrated Animal Encyclopedia. New York: The Macmillan Company, 1982.

Field Guides: Field guides are intended primarily to aid in the identification of animals living in specific areas. Some deal only with certain groups of animals, such as mammals, birds, fish, or insects. The guides tend to be organized on a regional basis, such as states, specific areas of the country, or special habitats. A description of each animal and some natural history are usually included. The following are examples of field guides:

Audubon Society Field Guides.   New York: Alfred A. Knopf. Series includes guides on insects and spiders, seashore creatures, fishes, reptiles and amphibians, birds, and mammals.

Golden Guides.   New York: Western Publishing Co. Series includes guides on insects, reptiles and amphibians, fishes, birds, and mammals.

Harper & Row's Complete Field Guide to North American Wildlife.   New York: Harper & Row Publishers, Inc.

The Peterson Field Guide Series.   Boston: Houghton Mifflin Company. Series includes guides on insects, reptiles and amphibians, birds, and mammals.

Magazines

A number of magazines regularly feature articles about animals. Some magazines are targeted for young readers; others provide useful background for teachers, including photographs of animals that can be shared with students. Magazines for students and teachers include the following:

For Students:

National Geographic World.   Published by the National Geographic Society, 17th and M Sts., N.W., Washington, D.C. 20036. For ages 8–13.

Owl.   Published by the Young Naturalist Foundation, P.O. Box 1700, Buffalo, NY 14271. For ages 7–14.

Ranger Rick.   Published by the National Wildlife Federation, 1412 16th St., N.W., Washington, D.C. 20036. For ages 6–12.

For Teachers:

Audubon.   Published by the National Audubon Society, 950 Third Ave., New York, NY 10022.

International Wildlife.   Published by the National Wildlife Federation, 1412 16th St., N.W., Washington, D.C. 20036.

National Geographic.   Published by the National Geographic Society, 17th and M Sts., N.W., Washington, D.C. 20036.

National Wildlife.   Published by the National Wildlife Federation, 1412 16th St., N.W., Washington, D.C. 20036.

Natural History.   Published by the American Museum of Natural History, Central Park W. at 79th St., New York, NY 10024

Ranger Rick's NatureScope.   Published by the National Wildlife Federation, 1412 16th St., N.W., Washington, D.C. 20036

Science and Children.   Published by the National Science Teachers Association, 1742 Connecticut Ave., N.W., Washington, D.C. 20009.

Audio-Visuals

There are many films, filmstrips, and video cassettes about animals, their lives, and their habitats. These audio-visual materials may be available through school, local, or regional libraries. Many films are also available on a loan or rental basis from a variety of sources that can usually be located through libraries. Audio-visual materials can also be purchased through some biological supply companies (see Commercial Suppliers, next page) and through media producers and distributors. Some examples of media companies are:

Coronet/MTI Film & Video Distributors of LCA, 108 Wilmot Rd., Deerfield, IL 60015

Encyclopaedia Britannica Educational Corp., 425 N. Michigan Ave., Chicago, IL 60611

Guidance Associates, Communications Park, Box 3000, Mount Kisco, NY 10549

National Geographic Society, Educational Services, Box 85, 17th and M Sts., N.W., Washington, D.C. 20036

United Learning, 6633 W. Howard St., Niles, IL 60648

Museums, Nature Centers, Universities, and Zoos

In addition to the excellent learning opportunities afforded by visits to nature centers, zoos, college or university science departments, and museums, many of these organizations conduct educational programs. These programs vary considerably, depending on the size and purpose of the organization, but some include a variety of courses and publications, the loan of materials and films, visiting naturalists, and, in some cases, traveling animal exhibits.

National, Regional, and Local Organizations

Some nature organizations offer a variety of educational materials, such as books, films, posters, animal identification flash cards, and pamphlets, that can be used to enhance animal study programs. Many communities also have a local nature study or conservation club that sometimes has a national affiliation and thus access to a variety of resources.

Examples of national nature organizations are:

National Audubon Society, 950 Third Ave., New York, NY 10022.

National Geographic Society, 17th and M Sts., N.W., Washington, D.C. 20036.

National Wildlife Federation, 1412 16th St., N.W., Washington, D.C. 20036.

Commercial Suppliers

Many animals and the supplies needed to care for them are available from local sources. Pet stores or pet centers in department stores are good sources of animals, cages, animal food, and information. Materials for constructing cages can be obtained from hardware stores and lumber companies, and much of the food needed for small animals can be purchased from bait shops, feed companies, and supermarkets.

Biological Supply Companies: Many biological supply companies also offer classroom animals and supplies on a mail-order basis. (Most will send teachers catalogs upon request.) Examples of companies that cater to schools are:

Carolina Biological Supply Company, 2700 York Rd., Burlington, NC 27215 *or* Box 187, Gladstone, OR 97027

Connecticut Valley Biological Supply Co., Inc., 82 Valley Rd., P.O. Box 326, Southhampton, MA 01073

Fisher Scientific, Educational Materials Division, 4901 W. LeMoyne St., Chicago, IL 60651

Kons Scientific Co., Inc., P.O. Box 3, Germantown, WI 53022–0003

Nasco, 901 Janesville Ave., Fort Atkinson, WI 53538 *or* P.O. Box 3837, 1524 Princeton Ave., Modesto, CA 95352

Ward's Natural Science Establishment, Inc., 5100 West Henrietta Rd., P.O. Box 92912, Rochester, NY 14692–9012 *or* 11850 East Florence Ave., P.O. Box 2567, Santa Fe Springs, CA 90670–0567

People

Probably every community has people who are willing to share their experiences and knowledge of animals with children. These people might include hobbyists who raise rabbits, pigeons, tropical fish, or other animals; farmers; veterinarians; college or university personnel; pet store owners; conservation officers; naturalists; 4-H and conservation club members; school district science coordinators and teachers; and any other interested people with knowledge to share.

State Wildlife Agencies

Information on laws regulating the capture or importation of live animals can be obtained from the following wildlife agencies in the United States and Canada:

United States

ALABAMA Commissioner, Dept. of Conservation & Natural Resources, 64 N. Union St., Montgomery, AL 36104

ALASKA Commissioner, Dept. of Fish & Game, P.O. Box 3-2000, Juneau, AK 99802

ARIZONA Director, Game & Fish Dept., 2222 W. Greenway Rd., Phoenix, AZ 85023

ARKANSAS Director, Game & Fish Comm., #2 Natural Resources Dr., Little Rock, AR 72205

CALIFORNIA Director, Dept. of Fish & Game, 1416 Ninth St., Sacramento, CA 95814

COLORADO Director, Div. of Wildlife, Dept. of Natural Resources, 6060 Broadway, Denver, CO 80216

CONNECTICUT Chief, Dept. of Environmental Protection, Division of Conservation and Preservation, 165 Capitol Ave., Hartford, CT 06106

DELAWARE Director, Div. of Fish & Wildlife, Natural Resources & Environmental Control, P.O. Box 1401, Dover, DE 19903

FLORIDA Director, Game & Fresh Water Fish Comm., Dept. of Natural Resources, 620 S. Meridian St., Tallahassee, FL 32301

GEORGIA Director, Game & Fish Div., Dept. of Natural Resources, 205 Butler St., S.W., Atlanta, GA 30334

HAWAII Director, Land & Natural Resources Dept., 1151 Punchbowl St., Honolulu, HI 96813

IDAHO Director, Dept. of Fish & Game, 600 S. Walnut St., P.O. Box 25, Boise, ID 83707

ILLINOIS Director, Dept. of Conservation, Lincoln Towers Plaza, 524 S. Second St., Springfield, IL 62706

INDIANA Director, Fish & Wildlife Div., Dept. of Natural Resources, 607 State Office Bldg., Indianapolis, IN 46204

Iowa   Administrator, Fish & Wildlife Div., Dept. of Natural Resources, Wallace State Office Bldg., Des Moines, IA 50319

Kansas   Director, Fish & Game Comm., Rt. 2, Box 54A, Pratt, KS 67124

Kentucky   Commissioner, Fish & Wildlife Dept., #1 Game Farm Rd., Frankfort, KY 40601

Louisiana   Secretary, Wildlife & Fisheries Dept., P.O. Box 15570, Baton Rouge, LA 70895

Maine   Commissioner, Dept. of Inland Fisheries & Wildlife, State House Station #41, Augusta, ME 04333

Maryland   Administrator, Tidewater Admn., Dept. of Natural Resources, Tawes State Office Bldg., Annapolis, MD 21401

Massachusetts   Director, Dept. of Fisheries, Wildlife & Recreational Vehicles, 100 Cambridge St., Boston, MA 02202

Michigan   Director, Dept. of Natural Resources, Mason Bldg., P.O. Box 30028, Lansing, MI 48909

Minnesota   Director, Div. of Fish & Wildlife, Dept. of Natural Resources, 500 Lafayette Rd., St. Paul, MN 55146

Mississippi   Director, Fisheries & Wildlife Bureau, Dept. of Wildlife Conservation, Southport Mall, Jackson, MS 39209

Missouri   Director, Dept. of Conservation, 2901 W. Truman Blvd., P.O. Box 180, Jefferson City, MO 65102

Montana   Director, Dept. of Fish, Wildlife & Parks, 1420 E. Sixth Ave., Helena, MT 59620

Nebraska   Director, Game & Parks Comm., 2200 N. 33rd St., P.O. Box 30370, Lincoln, NE 68503

Nevada   Director, Dept. of Wildlife, P.O. Box 10678, Reno, NV 89520

New Hampshire   Director, Fish & Game Dept., 34 Bridge St., Concord, NH 03301

New Jersey   Director, Fish, Game & Wildlife Div., Environmental Protection Dept., CN400, Trenton, NJ 08625

New Mexico   Director, Game & Fish Dept., Villagra Bldg., Santa Fe, NM 87503

New York   Commissioner, Dept. of Environmental Conservation, 50 Wolf Rd., Albany, NY 12233

North Carolina   Executive Director, Wildlife Resources Comm., Natural Resources & Community Development, 512 N. Salisbury St., Raleigh, NC 27611

North Dakota   Commissioner, Game & Fish Dept., 100 N. Bismarck Expwy., Bismarck, ND 58501

OHIO   Chief, Div. of Wildlife, Dept. of Natural Resources, Fountain Sq., Bldg. C-4, Columbus, OH 43224

OKLAHOMA   Director, Dept. of Wildlife Conservation, 1801 N. Lincoln Blvd., Oklahoma City, OK 73105

OREGON   Director, Dept. of Fish & Wildlife, 506 SW Mill St., Portland, OR 97201

PENNSYLVANIA   Executive Director, Game Comm., 8000 Derry St., Harrisburg, PA 17120

RHODE ISLAND   Chief, Fish & Wildlife Div., Dept. of Environmental Mgt., Washington County Govt. Ctr., South Kingstown, RI 02903

SOUTH CAROLINA   Executive Director, Wildlife & Marine Resources Dept., P.O. Box 167, Columbia, SC 29202

SOUTH DAKOTA   Secretary, Dept. of Game, Fish & Parks, Anderson Bldg., Pierre, SD 57501

TENNESSEE   Executive Director, Wildlife Resources Agcy., P.O. Box 40747, Nashville, TN 37204

TEXAS   Executive Director, Parks & Wildlife Dept., 4200 Smith School Rd., Austin, TX 78744

UTAH   Director, Div. of Wildlife Resources, Dept. of Natural Resources & Energy, 1596 W. N. Temple, Salt Lake City, UT 84116

VERMONT   Commissioner, Dept. of Fish & Wildlife, Agcy. of Natural Resources, 103 S. Main St., Waterbury, VT 05676

VIRGINIA   Executive Director, Dept. of Game & Inland Fisheries, P.O. Box 11104, Richmond, VA 23230

WASHINGTON   Acting Director, Dept. of Wildlife, 600 N. Capitol Way, Olympia, WA 98504

WEST VIRGINIA   Chief, Div. of Wildlife Resources, Dept. of Natural Resources, State Capitol Complex, Bldg. 3, Charleston, WV 25305

WISCONSIN   Director, Bureau of Wildlife Mgt., Dept. of Natural Resources, P.O. Box 7921, Madison, WI 53707

WYOMING   Director, Game & Fish Comm., 5400 Bishop Blvd., Cheyenne, WY 82002

DISTRICT OF COLUMBIA   Administrator, Housing & Environmental Regulations, Dept. of Consumer & Regulatory Affairs, 614 H St., N.W., Washington, DC 20001

AMERICAN SAMOA   Director, Marine Resources, Pago Pago, AS 96799

NORTHERN MARIANA ISLANDS   Chief, Fish & Wildlife Div., Natural Resources Dept., Saipan, CM 96950

PUERTO RICO   Secretary, Dept. of Natural Resources, P.O. Box 5887, San Juan, PR 00906

VIRGIN ISLANDS   Commissioner, Dept. of Planning & Natural Resources, #79 Altona & Welgunst, St. Thomas, VI 00802

Canada
(Provincial Offices)

ALBERTA   Fish & Wildlife Div., Dept. of Lands and Forests, Edmonton, Alberta

BRITISH COLUMBIA   Chief, Game Mgt., Fish & Game Br., Parliaments Bldg., Victoria, British Columbia

MANITOBA   Director of Wildlife, Dept. of Mines and Natural Resources, Winnipeg, Manitoba

NEW BRUNSWICK   Chief, Fish & Wildlife Br., Dept. of Lands and Mines, Fredericton, New Brunswick

NEWFOUNDLAND   Director of Wildlife, Dept. of Mines, Agriculture, and Resources, St. Johns, Newfoundland

NORTHWEST TERRITORIES   Deputy Commissioner of N.W.T., Vimy Bldg., Ottawa, Ontario

NOVA SCOTIA   Fish & Game Association, P.O. Box 654, Halifax, Nova Scotia

ONTARIO   Chief, Fish & Wildlife Br., Dept. of Lands and Forests, Parliaments Bldg., Toronto, Ontario

PRINCE EDWARD ISLAND   Director of Fish & Wildlife, Dept. of Industry & Natural Resources, Charlottetown, Prince Edward Island

QUEBEC   Director of Wildlife Div., Dept. of Tourism, Game and Fish, Quebec, Quebec

SASKATCHEWAN   Director of Wildlife, Dept. of Natural Resources, Government Admin. Bldg., Regina, Saskatchewan

YUKON TERRITORY   Game Dept., Yukon Territory, Whitehorse, Yukon Territory

Index